Dudesong

by

Phil Wells

ABIDE UNIVERSITY PRESS
DUDEISM.COM/AUP

2012

Dudesong

By Phil Wells

Copyright © 2012 Phil Wells. All Rights Reserved.
Printed in the United States of America

Cover Designer: J Hobart B

Printing History:
       September 2011   First Edition.

ISBN: 978-0-615-70174-5

This book would not have been possible without support from Ali Farahnakian and Desiree Nash at Simple Studios, the best place to rehearse (and work as a poet/doorman) in Manhattan.

Thanks to Toni from Queens for her fluency in Italian, and for her letting me borrow the same.

Finally, of course, thanks go to my wife Allison for her patience during the completion of this work. She's the best.

About Abide University Press

Despite the awesome-sounding name, Abide University Press is not a publishing house. Rather, we are a stamp of approval for books which we feel help promote the philosophy of Dudeism.

Books selected by Abide University press are self-published by their authors but promoted at Abide University, the educational wing of The Church of the Latter-Day Dude (Dudeism).

For more information, please visit us at abideuniversity.com/press.

Thankie.

Foreword

Joel Coen has gone on record saying that every movie is essentially a remake of "The Wizard of Oz." That is, they're all about someone just trying to get back home after taking a wrong turn somewhere. But as masters of cinema, the Coen brothers are obliged not to betray their industry. Long before moving pictures it was generally accepted that all stories are just remakes of Homer's Odyssey. Dororthy's quest for "no place like home" is also just an echo of Odysseus, that distant relative of Donald Kerabatsos. Every story is an odyssey. Were you listening to the Ode's story?

The Big Lebowski is no exception. The plot of The Big Lebowski was so unconventional that it confused critics for a decade, it too is a riff on Homer. Like Odysseus and Dorothy, the Dude gets lured and lost, spending the bulk of the story trying to find his way back home. On his journey he too discovers that though the world beyond his home may be filled with seductions, it is also filled with illusions, red herrings, deceptions, and pointless idealism.

Dudesong, Phil Wells' Homeric interpretation of The Big Lebowski is not the first work to reinterpret this Coen brothers masterpiece via an older idiom. Or rather, it may have been, but Adam Bertocci's wonderful Shakespearean rendition, Two Gentlemen of Lebowski beat it to the punch in the memeosphere and ultimately on the printed page. On the exact day that Wells put his pen down after ten months of crafting the book while moonlighting as a security guard, the Two Gentlemen meme burst out on the Internet, securing a book deal for Bertocci and a certain degree of frustration for Wells. Dude minds do think alike, after all, but Bertocci had the winds of fate against his sails.

But so what? Did Odysseus give up each time he got shipwrecked? Did Dorothy throw in the towel when she found herself trapped in Oz? Did the Dude sink into despair when he misplaced a million dollars? Well, yes, he did a bit. But then: "Can't be worried about that shit. Life goes on man!"

Perhaps after his year sailing between Dudeism and Delphi, this lesson of steadfastness (a.k.a. Abiding) had gotten under Wells' skin. So he too kept shuffling on ahead, publishing Dudesong line by line via Twitter and abiding his time until conditions were more favorable to release the craft onto the high seas.

If there's one thing that Lebowski (and the Odyssey, and Oz) teaches us, it's to step back from our own troubles and take in the big picture. All stories are only pit stops in a much bigger tale: the story of humankind. Wells' masterful mashup of Homer and the Coens drives this point home just as James Joyce did in his remake (Ulysses) and the Coens themselves did in O Brother Where Art Thou? That is: no matter how cloaked behind style and genre and artistic subterfuge, there is really only one story that has been told time and time again in various ways throughout history, and that is this: The Dude Abides. Even if we get sidetracked, there is in all of us a homing instinct towards a "home" in the universe. Sometimes it just takes us a while to get there.

We welcome this opportunity to congratulate Phil Wells on the release of this immodest achievement. As you will soon see, it is a marvelous and worthy offspring of two epic greatnesses. May he arrive at many more such Ithacas in his own creative odyssey.

Rev. Oliver Benjamin

Chiang Mai, Thailand 2012

CHAPTER I

Take heed before our minstrels start to play;
Some thoughts about the city of L.A.
The angels, this metropolis their home,
Kick tumbleweeds around the streets they roam.
From far across the desert sweaty slog
They trudge and bear across their backs the smog.
The stars above in absence dim the mood
Of all th'angelic stars in Hollywood;
Their lack reflects th'ambitions of our Dude.
Alas this cowboy finds himself ahead
Of this here story's glorious nar'tive thread.
"The Dude" was not thus by his parents called,
But "Jeff Lebowski" was the name they 'nstalled.

And this Lebowski, with peculiar taste,
Discarded "Jeff" and left "Dude" in its place.
You mustn't ask this cowboy why he'd switch
Aside to say it keeps my stories rich.
The Dude, this city, both to me so strange,
Afford this poem a home out on the range.
Before 2000 turned our hard drives back,
And Bush the Senior clobbered through Iraq
(And then his son decided to go back),
The Dude was set upon by happenstance,
And found himself a hurricane by chance.
And if the Fates had luck enough to lend,
They bet The Dude he'd live to see the end.
Be stupefied as I begin to tell
Just how The Dude precipitously fell
And played the hero climbin' outta Hell.
The only thing that makes a hero great
Is how he plays the hand he's dealt by Fate.
The Dude, it seemed, fit right into his time;
Los Angeles in decade number nine.
His laziness was not a factor when
The open door of life let chaos in.
When duty calls sometimes there is a man,
And 'twas The Dude who had become this man...

Aw Hell. I rambled on for much too long.
This introduction's over; here's the song.

CHAPTER II

At Ralph's the angels shop for things to eat,
The tiles a frozen lake beneath their feet.
The light all artificial burning down
In ambient majesty lights up the ground.
So late that only th' angels grace the aisles
And restless young cashiers that count the whiles.
This night there shopped a man, the angels' ilk;
The Dude had stopped inside to grab some milk.
He stooped and grabbed it slow, though hardly tired,
And drank a bit to see if it'd expired.
Then satisfied he found an express line;
A check to pay his tab, oh-point-six-nine

(The Dude's Ralph's discount card saved him a dime).
And all the time the TV played the news:
"This aggression will not stand," the Prez construed,
"This will not stand," said Bush with rage again;
A mask of strength t' intimidate Hussein.
From o'er his shades our hero took this in
Then left into the lot, his car therein.
The bagboy didn't know which car to pack;
"The Gran Torino," Dude said, "in the back."

At home, a jaunty jog up winded path,
The Dude direct'd his gait round birded bath,
And with his groc'ries and his bowling ball
Ascendt his steps and leant them on the wall,
Unlocked his door and walked into his home.
He could not tell that he was not alone.
The lights alit, he stepped into the room
While angels warned behind him, danger loomed.
He tried to turn, to look behind and see,
But first was caught 'n an armpit angrily.
The Dude was dragged with screams down darkened hall,
His heavy satchel swinging, splint'ring walls
Until at 'partment's end, the bathroom reached,
Our hero's head the toilet water breached.

The force with which The Dude had been so brought
Explod'd the milk into a creamy blot.
The screams, milk popping: all these sounds replaced
By toilet gurgling wrought by sunken face.
This thug then spoke to make 's intentions clear:
"We want the money, L'bowski, give it here!
From Bunny did we hear that you would pay
Her debts to Jackie Treehorn right away.
Your wife's in debt to him a tidy sum,
Give in and pay or a drowned man you'll become.
Your breath is catching now in tortured fits;
We want the money, shit-head! Where is it?"
With moments t' answer, Dude spat through the pain,
"It's down there somewhere. Let me look again."
So down and up his head was roughly lashed,
And o'er again into his toilet splashed
Until at last The Dude was tossed aside,
His glasses gone, eyes blinking as they dried.
Now looking up The Dude his foe surveyed:
Some roid-rage blond, his half-wet tank-top gray.
And there beyond in Th' Dude's own living room,
An Asian gent the size of mortal doom.
He watched this Chinese man with belt all slipped
Turn back and heard his bleachéd jeans unzip.

Then "Ever thus to deadbeats," said the thug
Who calmly peed an "X" into the rug.
"Don't do that, man," The Dude, resigned, began,
And donned his shades recovered from the can,
"Not on the rug," he begged then took a seat
While kicking milky water off his feet.
"Lebowski," blond intoned, "Can you not see?
This happens t' deadbeats, L'bowski; nothing's free."
"I'm not Lebowski, no one calls me that.
Call me The Dude," the soggy Duder spat.
"Your name's Lebowski, L'bowski. Bunny's y'r wife."
The Dude then gaped in honest disbelief.
He had no wife! These guys had found th' wrong man:
"D' you see a wedding ring upon this hand?
Have you not eyes to glance about the room
And see no work's been done with mop or broom?
Do you suppose this Bunny would lay by
As her own husband leaves the wash rags dry?
I'm not your man Lebowski; give it up.
My wife, you fools? The toilet seat is up!"
So blond looked down to see what Dude had brought:
Some groc'ries and his satchel packed all taut.
He stooped t' open the leather bag with gall,
Removed and held aloft a bowling ball,

And looked at this with all the puzzlement
'f a caveman introduced to steel and flint.
He asked, "The fuck is this?" to which Dude proffered,
"It's obvious that you are not a golfer."
The blond reviled and dropped the twelve-pound sphere;
Collapsing tiles screamed murder through the air.
"Hey Wu?" blond asked, to make sure this was clear,
"'s this guy supposed to be a millionaire?"
Big Wu and friend surveyed where they had hid
And tried t' descry how this Lebowski did.
Around them lay the muck of ages past:
Old clothes and milky tumblers all amassed,
Spent roaches and their ashes in the trays,
The taste of dust, the smell of mayonnaise,
And Ziploc bags of every shape and size
With all their priceless cannabis excised.
Now Wu began to realize with fright
That he and blond had wasted their whole night.
He zipped his jeans and called back testily,
"This guy looks like a fucking loser t' me."
The tranquil Dude peered o'er his sunglass frames
And said, "Hey man, at least I'm potty-trained."
A flustered exit served as their reply,
With "Thanks for nothing, asshole," their good-bye.

12

The Dude just sat atop his toilet, hushed,
And watched as out the door th' attackers rushed.
His stillness never once betrayed his fright;
He dragged the rug out to the curb that night.

When angels bowl they say the thunder rolls;
A deaf'ning sound to shake the mortal soul.
To think! With all that Heaven can arrange,
Untold delights to keep them entertained,
Its angels still return to bowling lanes.
Our Dude as well preferred that noble sport;
The sounds of bowling cut his worries short.
That murmur as the ball rolled down the wood,
The clatter of the pins if th' shot was good.
And from the P.A. speakers hung afar,
Bob Dylan from the jukebox in the bar:

The man in me will do nearly any task,
And as for compensation, there's little he would ask.
Take a woman like you
To get through to the man in me.
Storm clouds are raging all around my door,
I think to myself I might not take it anymore.
Take a woman like your kind

To find the man in me.
But, oh, what a wonderful feeling
Just to know that you are near,
Sets my heart a-reeling
From my toes up to my ears.
The man in me will hide sometimes to keep from bein' seen,
But that's just because he doesn't want to turn into some machine.
Took a woman like you
To get through to the man in me.

The Dude's home alley boasted thirty lanes,
Was family-owned, not part of some big chain,
And drinks and games were had till moonlight waned.
That night the place was packed with malcontents
All signing up for that week's tournament.
So far and wide the bowlers heaved their stones;
They dried their palms and cracked their knuckle bones
And spares and strikes they picked up by the tens;
Fist pumps and twists to celebrate their gains.
And every one fancied himself a champ
Till each went home, essentially a tramp.
Ten pins that night, defiant in their stance,
Stood down the lane where Donny did advance.
He threw his ball and watched the pins with hope

And all were cast aside in one fell swoop.
His face lit up in unrestrained delight:
"Dude, mark it ten. I'm throwing rocks tonight!"
He sauntered back to where The Dude was perched:
The scoring table near the players' bench.
The Dude had not heard Donny's glad report,
But was with Walter mired deep in thought.
"This rug," Walt said, "was not a useless scrap.
You treasured it before tonight's mishap."
The Dude drank beer and swallowed through the pain,
"It really tied the room together, man."
"This was a valued, uh..." Walt stopped to think.
"What did?" asked Donny, picking up his drink,
"What tied the room together, Dude?" he asked
And in an instant Walt was heard t' react:
"Were you around to hear The Dude explain
His story which has brought him naught but pain?"
"I had to bowl," said Donny to this test.
"You have no frame of ref'rence; you're a pest,"
Said Walter, "You are like a child, at best.
You'd wander in a movie 'nd want to know..."
"But Walter, what's the point?" Dude stopped his flow.
Still rolling, hardly knocked all out of joint,
"The point," Walt said, "Dude, here's the fucking point:

There is no reason, there's no fucking rea..."
"Yeah, what's your point?" asked Donny testily.
With this Walt was just for a moment stalled;
"What's that?" he asked of Donny, all appalled.
Then Dude took over: "What's the point of this?
We know the source of th' aforementioned piss.
With ease we can pinpoint the man at fault,
So what the fuck 're you talking 'bout, dear Walt?"
Annoyed with rage The Dude put on his shoes
As Walter sat up in his seat, bemused.
Walt tried to speak: "Not what the fuck are you..."
He raged, then stopped, then tried again anew:
"I'm not," he barked, then sat up straight again,
And searched his mind to make his meaning plain.
Now Walter spoke 'n his calmest timbre yet,
And gestured with his unlit cigarette:
"The subject here's aggression gone unchecked..."
"'t's he talking about?" asked Donny the perplexed.
"My rug," The Dude explained as Walter seethed,
And leaned too low and scowled too hard to breathe.
"Forget it, Donny," Walter bellowed then,
"You're out of your element," he cried again
(As angry now as Walt had ever been).
The Dude looked up from laces as he tied

And tried to prove that reason's on his side:
"Hey Walter, man, the Chinaman at fault
Is not tied up in my apartment, caught.
His whereabouts are no more known to I
Than th' number of all the angels in the sky.
If I should seek recompense for my rug
I've nary a billing address to reach the thug.
About this fact, no reason you should shout.
We're talking here, but what the fuck about?"
"The fuck about?" screamed Walter, talking quick
As neurons in his brain sparked on and clicked;
"I'm speaking of a line drawn in the sand.
On each side a combatant proudly stands.
The rules of justice, simple as you please:
Across this line, YOU DO NOT..." then, with ease,
"And also, Dude, when speaking of th' Chinese,
'Chinaman' is wrong; 'Asian-American', please."
"Fuck. Walter, man," said Dude with unpacked sphere,
"It's not a guy who built the railroads here.
My nomenclature fits this heinous dog.
We're talking 'bout a guy who pees on rugs."
What havoc may semantics play on fools!
Such slavery to grammar's haughty rules.
"The fuck are you...?" exploded Walt with ire,

Cut short by voices clam'ring to scream higher:
"He ruined my rug," said Dude, "with vile piss!"
"He ruined Dude's rug," did Donny add to this.
With all the rage of Spring's first hot foment
From Walter's maw came: "You're out of y'r element!"
And then, "The Chinaman's not the issue, Dude."
The Dude stood up and asked, "If not, then who?"
He strode from round the bench t' approach the lanes
And rolled his neck to clear his addled brains.
A man with answers sometimes waits till asked
To edify, and this was Walter's task:
"The Chinaman should be far from your mind
For visiting in manner unrefined.
You say the truth: he can no more repay
Than can the moon shine down at mid of day.
Your quarrel, Dude, is with Lebowski found
(The other Jeff Lebowski in this town).
He shares your name; past that one can't compare
For you're The Dude and he's a millionaire."
"That int'resting, man," The Dude said as he stretched
And pointed up at th' ceiling with his chest.
Said Walt, "This Jeff, whoever he may be,
Could not be hard to find, that's plain to see.
Seek out this man who clearly has the wealth,

and resources, and the financial health.
'Cause there's no reason, there's no fucking way,
His wife should owe his cash 'round town, I say.
She runs up debts and makes her husband poor.
These fuckers come and piss upon your floor?
The big Lebowski's your man. Am I wrong?"
Then Walt leaned back, his argument quite strong.
"Yeah, but..." asked Dude, so, "Am I wrong?" asked Walt,
"It really tied the room together, did 't not?"
"Yeah, Fucking A," The Dude affirmed through sips.
"And these guys peed on it," from Donny's lips.
Then "Donny, please," did Walter scold with haste
And rubbed an ash from 'bove his ample waist.
The Dude was set to bowl but made this clear:
"My time for justice surely must be near.
The Big Lebowski's wife has no more right
To run up debts than I've to run red lights.
The debt was hers; from me they would collect?
Likewise her man should feel their pee's effect.
I'll find this guy and he'll pay for repairs
To fix my rug, you know. It's only fair.
His wife owes cash to th' employer of these thugs;
They come around and pee upon my rug?"
Said Walt: "They peed upon your fucking rug."

Said Dude: "They peed upon my fucking rug."
Said Walt: "They peed upon your fucking rug."
Said Dude: "They peed upon my fucking rug."
Said Walt: "They peed upon your fucking rug."

CHAPTER III

Los Angeles itself could be explained
As two towns packed into just one's domain.
Just as the lanes may host a range of class,
So rich and poor in L.A. do amass.
Celebrities and playboys stake their lots
While shoeless ghouls sleep out of cars or cots.
The Dude himself, while not a man of means,
Was comfortable in most the city's scenes:
The bowling alley bars held no contempt,
From their guest lists The Dude was not exempt;
And similarly clubs and discotheques,
And poolside bars, and parties out on decks,

And dry bars set in corners of dry homes,
Plus fancy garden fetes with garden gnomes.
The Dude could fit right in to all of these;
His gentle attitude, his weed, his ease.
At present, though, The Dude did find himself
In an estate where top was every shelf
And nary a klatch 'round here was to be had
Save for the dance of duster by a maid.
Th' estate of Jeff Lebowski sprawled for miles,
All Monticello doorways, checkered tiles,
And nouveau accents hung on plaster walls,
And thrones and fresh-cut flow'rs adorned the halls.
The Dude surveyed the study with L'bowski's man;
This Brandt had zero clue and zero tan.
A micro pattern tie and pressed blue suit,
No detail out of place or too minute.
An automatic door had let them in
So Brandt's fond presentation could begin:
"We enter now the study where one finds
Awards and plaques of several various kinds,
Degrees from schools where geniuses have learned,
Certificates that Mr. L'bowski's earned.
Inspect them, Dude! You're welcome! Be my guest!
(I'll not let you deny this wee request)"

23

The Dude politely balked, his steps retraced
But Brandt insisted and went on, apace:
"You must see this! I see you spy this key
The town of Pasadena gave to he
For sundry duties: civic, otherwise...
Ah, but, alas, I see you've turned your eyes
Toward L.A.'s most respected public prize:
The Chamb'r of Commerce Business Acheiv'r Award!
A shining highlight 'mong his prizéd hoard.
Yes that award is given every year--
Well, not some years, which makes it much more dear--
Just years when someone worthy, someone staid..."
As Brandt would rant The Dude removed his shades,
"This pic with Nancy; is this your boss here?"
"It is, indeed, and just to make it clear..."
From pic to Brandt the Duder's vision cleft,
"This one's Lebowski, seated on the left?"
And Brandt, stopped short, was made but more uptight,
"Of course he is. And Nancy's on the right."
This caught The Dude completely unaware;
The pictured man was confined to a chair!
(A curious state for a fucking millionaire)
"So he's a crip .. uh, I mean .. that is to say ..
Your boss is made to live his life this way?"

Brandt understood and answered then with tact:
"He is disabled. Yes, that is a fact.
As this shot here was taken, by the way,
She was First Lady of the USA,
Not just of California, sir. Yes, yes?
And I believe it'd hold your interest
That Ronald w's also met along this stop
Though, sadly, too briefly for a photo op."
"Oh, Nancy's pretty good," The Dude surmised.
"Oh, wonderful, yes! We all were hypnotized,
Spellbound by th' Lady's presence; held in place!
No mere photographer could catch her grace."
The Dude paced on and Brandt stayed by his side,
His words a constant stream as they descried
Among the wall of plaques and framed degrees
More pics of th' man beside celebrities:
Here he and Charlton Heston exchangéd smiles.
"Far out," The Dude observed 's he walked the tiles.
Their footsteps and Brandt's chatter filled the room
Which otherwise'd be cold, still as a tomb.
Then plaques and plaques and soon they came upon
A shot of him with twenty urban spawn.
Asked Dude, "These kids, uh .. what's the deal with them?"
And Brandt, cut off mid-thought replied, "Ahem.

25

Oh those are L'bowski's children, so to speak..."

"I see. I guess that he's cool racially?"

"They're not..." squawked Brandt, who'd seemed to 've lost the thread.

"From different mothers, huh?" The Dude misread.

"Oh ha ha ha," laughed Brandt, to interrupt,

"They're lit'rally not his," he blushed, abrupt,

"It's Little L'bowski Urb'n Achievers seen.

Poor kids without the necessary means for

Necessary means for college costs,

So their tuition's paid for by my boss.

Excuse me!" Brandt admonished, growing tense,

Because The Dude had touched an ornamence.

"With all these kids d' you think there's any place

For one more smiling, grant-receiving face?"

"One more..? Oh ha ha ha, I see," said Brandt,

"You've never cried an alma mater chant,

Or earned a credit in a college course?

Your education's high school lev'l or worse."

Then Brandt reached out his arm and primly shooed

The Dude, who'd poked again a bronzéd shoe.

"Oh yeah, I went," The Dude explained with pride,

"'Twas there all those old halls I occupied.

We'd sit in paths where bursars tried to pass

And offer them a flower or some hash."
(Once more the Duder poked the mounted stash).
"Smoked thai stick, broke into th'ROTC,
And bowled a lot whenever I was free.
(At least so says my porous memory)."
By then he'd turned a corner in that place
And stopped before a painted looking glass
Made up to look like "Time" the magazine;
"Are You A L'bowski Achiever?" in it, silk-screened.
The captions so adroitly framed Dude's face
He shambled, slowed, and stopped his glacial pace.
He stared, transfixed, at himself, th' man of th' year
When all at once there screamed a grind of gears,
A whir of servos, clatt'ring wooden doors,
And wheelchair wheels squeaked over creaking floors.
The Dude and Brandt both turned to face the noise
And saw the man in motion, yet reg'lly poised.
Fat old Lebowski, 's he rolled his person in,
Had hardly paused a moment to begin:
"All right. I'm here. Your host has now arrived.
I know how long of me you've been deprived.
That's not my style; I'm just a busy man,
As I imagine you, as well, take pains.
So let us start and end this talk with haste:

You're a Lebowski, I'm a Lebowski. Great!
So how may I help you?" the codger asked
's he found his way behind an oaken desk.
This man filled th' room; larger than life he seemed,
His scowl a falls o'er which his grumbles teemed.
Dismissed, Brandt left, as a shadow'd at mid-day
And closed the doors behind him on his way.
A chair before Lebowski's desk was set
And it was there The Dude's intent was met.
Not all nonplussed but calm he crossed the room.
Dude casually spake as toward that chair he loomed:
"Well sir, the rug's the issue as it stands.
It really tied the room together, man."
At that, Dude sat, and crossed his legs at ease;
His flannel shorts betrayed his bowler's knees.
"Before you came, you told Brandt on the phone
And he told me, so all of this is known.
These things you say, I have been made aware.
You may go on, but wherefore should I care?"
All this Lebowski barked; The Dude took pause,
And wondered at this ire and its cause.
With patience then and logic 'e forged ahead
And on one knee let rest the other leg:
"Well these two guys were looking for your home

But to my place'd they accidentally roam..."
And that, he guessed, was that. What need be said
Beyond the facts so plain in Duder's head?
Lebowski shifted then, and took great pain
To make his words sounds sharp, his language plain:
"I'll say once more, I know what befell thee.
You told Brandt on the phone and he told me.
I know your tale, I'll not hear it again.
Get on with it, I say, my patience wanes."
But now The Dude could read between the lines;
The tone and body language were as signs.
This moneybag had no intent to pay
So it was up to Dude his will to sway.
"Oh, so you know the things that I have seen?
And on whose rug those fuckers should have peen?"
Lebowski, though, was proving pretty keen.
"Did I pee on your rug?" he asked point blank
And for a moment Dude just sat and thank.
"When you ask that, should I take it to mean
If you, yourself, my rug made a latrine?"
Right then he pictured how such 'n act would look;
This guy roll'ng into place in Dude's front nook
And clamb'ring down in phases from his chair
To pee up as a fountain in the air.

"Hello!" Jeff yelped, "Do you speak English well?
Ou parlez-vous Anglais, mademoiselle?
I'll say again, though 't pains me to repeat:
Did I abuse your rug like a toilet seat?"
How can one answer such a blatant ploy?
What logic could The Dude hope to employ?
"No, as I said before it wasn't you;
The pee'r was this other guy named Wu."
Lebowski splayed his hand to halt The Dude
And pointed then to make himself more rude:
"I want to understand, to get this straight.
Now every time on rugs thugs micturate
'n Los Angeles I have to compensate?"
And like a principal'd dress down a child
The Big Lebowski raged, his eyes gone wild.
'Twas all The Dude could do to interrupt,
"Come on," he plead, and stopped his foe abrupt,
"I didn't come to scam you, so relent.
You've got all wrong my innocent intent."
Lebowski scowled and swallowed his disgust
And hulked mid-chair 's his next barrage was thrust:
"Are you employed, Mr. Lebowski, sir?"
With feignéd resignation did he slur.
This all o'ertook The Dude as would the tides.

"I must explain," he said, and wiped his eyes,
"I'm not Mr. Lebowski as you claim
But you are he; Lebowski is your name.
I am The Dude so you should call me that
Or Duder, or His Dudeness (that's ornate),
Or if the soul 'f your wit's not brevity,
El Duderino might with you agree."
This quip did not amuse the larger man
Who rolled his eyes and started in again:
"Are you employed now sir?" he condescent.
The Dude caught up. "Employed?" his voice he bent.
"I hope," Lebowski said, "that you don't lurk
In clothes like those when looking for some work."
He pointed at The Dude and, like a bray,
"You meet the world like this on a weekday?"
By this assault and by the question stunned,
Dude looked around the room, his mind out-cunned.
"Is this a week...?" he started, then he stopped,
"What day is this?" he squeaked through sweat he'd flopped.
This had dragged on and for fresh air L. pined;
"I do work, sir. So if you do not mind..."
And he commenced to wheel himself around
When Dude, incensed, lashed out with plaintive sound:
"No, look! I mind, you know? The Duder minds!

I've been put out in ways of sundry kinds.
You might be th' richest guy in all the land
But simply put, this 'gression will not stand!
You think this fair? Your wife goes out and owes..."
"MY WIFE," Lebowski thundered, loud as Jove
And slammed his fist so hard down on his desk
All th' angels in the room made their egress,
"By God, my wife is not the issue here.
I'll thank you not to deign to interfere.
My hope is one day she can learn to live
On th' ample allowance I am wont to give.
I take great pains to make sure she lives well,
For all her gains, she thinks her Heaven's Hell.
If she cannot adapt and see the light
The problem then is hers, and hers outright.
It isn't mine to take upon her lot;
She's her own person whe'er she earns or not.
And just as her frivolity is hers,
Your spoiled rug is hardly mine, but yours.
And likewise every bum with problems hence
Shall not pollute my court with evidence
And all their problems they will solely own.
I'm not their charity, their chaperon.
I'd never grace your gutter t' blame the dregs

For th' total loss and crippling of my legs.
Some Chinaman 'n Korea took them away.
But I went out and achieved anyway!
I cannot solve your problems sir, it's true.
The only one who'll help you now is you."
With stoic face The Dude heard this tirade
And halfway through he re-put on his shades.
He shrugged his hands as he uncrossed his gams.
"Ah, fuck it," said he then (he gave no damns).
Half-heartedly he took stock in his chair:
His shades, his clothes; yep, everything was there.
Lebowski griped, "Oh, fuck it! Yes, of course!
That's your reply for everything, your curse!
Tattoo it on your forehead, might as well!
You'd never have to speak again at all."
The Dude had risen, turned, commenced to go;
Lebowski undeterred raged on like so:
"Your revolution's over sir; it's tossed!
Condolences, good sir. The bums have lost!
If I were one for guidance I'd advise
You seek the path your parents realized:
Go get a job! You bum! You dank refuse!
Your way is dead. The bum will always lose!
I pray you hear me through the dope and booze!

It's hopeless, sir! The bums will always--"

The Dude had slammed the door and left that place.
Now with a massive hallway he was faced.
He paced himself 's he strolled the marble floor
While Brandt advanced and shouted to implore:
"I trust your meeting ended rather well?
I'd left the room so I can scarcely tell.
You're strolling now and beaming with a glow.
Mr. Lebowski, tell me, how'd it go?"
With hands in pockets, Zen from head to feet,
The Dude responded, not missing a beat:
"Your boss, the champ, was grandly generous;
Said I could take home any rug in th' house."

And so it was; The Dude had claimed his right
And chose a rug with patterns nice and tight,
A Persian thing that just fit out the door
But when unrolled would dress The Duder's floor.
He walked with Brandt along a mezzanine
That overlooked the pool and yards of green.
Behind them came the rug rolled up and safe
Borne by a gardener on Lebowski's staff.
Anon they heard a radio's tinny blare

And bossa nova music filled the air.
It amplified as Dude this garden stalked
While jabb'ring Brandt b'lathered as they walked:
"Well Dude, enjoy! And please again stop by."
Such pleasantries as th' music waxed nearby.
"Oh yeah," said Dude, "I might just take that on
'f I'm in the niehgb'rhood, need to use the john..."
By then the music's source had been made clear:
A woman lounged and listened on this tier.
She faced away from where Dude 'proached with pace
(He'd seen enough to not need see her face).
All blonde and tan she bopped there in her chair,
The back of her bikini touched by 'r hair.
They were upon her then, her face was seen
Just as she finished painting 'r toenails green.
Her shades were low across her perfect nose
Which wrinkled cutely and she wiggled toes.
Brandt, who'd walked on a bit behind her chair,
And Dude who'd stopped at 'r feet to rightly stare,
Both men now stood and needed her to speak
Before they'd carry on and Dude's car seek.
(The gard'ner stopped too, was thankful for a break).
This babe reclined with comfort in her chaise
And toward Dude's face her tinted toenails raised.

"Blow on them," she said 's he took her foot
In a way that moved The Duder to his root.
Her toes with cotton balls tucked in between
Had been meticulously painted green.
"You want me to..." he started, sounding struck,
As if he hardly could believe his luck,
"Blow on your toes?" he finished to be sure.
"Uh huh," she giggled, "I can't blow that far."
The Dude had not expected this at all.
What girl was this outside Lebowski's walls?
He leaned his head to blow, but heard a splash;
From yonder in the pool a loner washed.
There floated on a raft a man in black
(Though only trunks, with no shirt on his back).
He dozed mid-pool, his paleness glowing white.
Nearby a whiskey bottle floated, light.
And though this guy was gone-zo to the world,
He could've been an item with this girl.
"But will he mind?" The Dude asked o'er his shades
An eyebrow cocked, still gripping th' lady's jades.
"Oh, he won't mind," she said, "I won't be missed.
My Uli cares for naught, 's a nihilist."
"Poor guy," said Dude, "exhausting life, that is..."
The lady smiled, absorbed this hipster's charms;

"You aren't blowing," coyly she alarmed.
She flexed her flipper lightly in his hand
Which turned him back to follow her command.
Now Brandt had seen enough of this chaise show:
"Madame Lebowski, our guest has to go."
So she withdrew her foot and changed her mood.
"You're Bunny?" asked the ever-curious Dude.
It now made sense, The Dude had figured all.
This wife's another plaque to grace the wall.
A trophy on the lawn to let th' world know
Lebowski had achieved. His prize? This doe.
Then Bunny doffed her shades, her knees in hugs;
"I'll suck your cock for just a thousand bucks."
At this proposal, purposely uncouth,
A hurricane of laughs blew from Brandt's mouth.
He grew so tense his shoulders ate his neck
And flapped his arms as would a nervous drake.
"Ha ha! Ha ha! A wonderful woman, yes?
So free in spirit, t' exhibit such largesse!
The staff and I, we all have grown quite fond..."
Then Bunny cut him off 'fore he went on:
"But Brandt can't watch unless a hundred's paid."
With serious demeanor she relayed.
"That's marvelous," said Brandt through more forced laughs

And led the way away on Dude's behalf.
From o'er his shoulder Dude called to the queen,
"I'm going now to find a cash machine."
As Brandt showed him into a limousine.
So Bunny watched him go and dried her nails,
While Uli in the pool dreamed dreams (all pale).

CHAPTER IV

Back at the lanes another round was played
'n an official game to see who'd move ahead.
'Twas Donny's turn; he rolled with studied ease
And all pins were upended as he pleased.
He made a fist and pumped it down but once,
And smiling turned to face the scorer's bench.
He hooted then and looked o'er at his foes,
Still beaming as he pointed and cajoled,
"You guy are dead 'n the water," Donny bragged;
The Dude's high-five, then offered, Donny tagged.
For th' opposing side was Smokey's turn up next
And just then Walter strolled upon the decks.

"All right now, Donny! That is how you play!"
Said Walter, "Keep that up; we'll win the day!
Our championship's now closer than it seems
For if you will it, then it is no dream."
Walt sat beside The Dude and shirked his load:
His ball 'nd a pet case whence yaps did explode.
With practiced nonchalance he placed this crate
As Dude griped "Man, you're twenty minutes late."
Then "What the fuck is that?" The Dude pressed on.
"That's Theodore Herzel," Walt said, "sine qua non.
The being of the state of Israel rests with he
for if you will it, Dude, it is no drea..."
"No, what the fuck..." snapped Dude 's he sipped his bock,
"Not that! The carrier! What's that in the box?"
As Walt untied his shoes he realized
The carrier was not hid from prying eyes.
Still, calm as church mice, Walt made dialogue:
"Oh that. This here is Cynthia's little dog.
Its breed is Pomeranian, so I think
(You know it's thus because its tongue is pink)."
As Dude protested, Walter loosed the beast
Which was a shih-tzu, native to the East.
It scampered from its cage and sniffed around
And took great interest when Dude's feet were found.

Said Walt, "While Cynthia has gone away
With Ackerman t' Hawaii for some days,
I have agreed to watch her treasured pet."
The Dude was not thus satisfied just yet.
"You brought it bowling?" Dude asked 'bout the pup,
His beer all low and his impatience up.
Walt said, "Now 'brought it bowling' I'd not say,
For this dog has no plans to roll today
And furthermore I will not rent it shoes
For, look! Its paws are far too numerous.
If I had brought it bowling, one would think,
I'd owe it beer or something else to drink.
And let me say, to vanquish your concern,
I promise not to let it take your turn."
The Dude surveyed the beast with bald distaste
Not for the dog, but for Walt's love misplaced.
Said Dude, "Man, if my ex-wife flew away
To Honolulu with her new fiancé,
I'd not be one to watch her fucking dog.
Why can't you board the mangy little pug?"
This Walter, with The Dude, was always calm
And civ'lly he addressed his best friend's qualm:
"Well, first of all, you haven't got an ex,
And as for boarding this dog's too complex.

'f I board this dog its fucking hair falls out;
A costly mishap, that you shouldn't doubt.
It's not some common cur, I'll have you know.
This dog's got fucking papers. It's for show."
"Hey man," The Dude was 'bout to interject
While Walter's head turned slowly on its neck.
Walt scanned the room; perhaps he could survey
Some kind divergence t' cause this chat's delay.
"The fucking dog has fucking papers, Dude,"
He said, then yowled, his temperament unglued,
With "O'ER THE LINE!" he filled the clam'ring hall;
A shot he'd aimed at Smokey, heard by all.
With startled sheepishness then Smokey turned
To see 'f the source of this could be discerned.
His silver hair was pushed back in long wisps;
"What's that?" he asked through meek yet playful lisps.
So Walter reasserted, "Sorry, Smoke.
But in your previous roll a rule was broke.
When you stepped o'er the line it was a foul.
Sit down. We're up. It's our turn next to bowl."
His foe dismissed, it seemed, Walt tied his shoes
But Smokey said "Bullshit!" He would not lose,
"Dude, mark it eight," he ordered boastfully.
The turn of phrase made Walt blush toastily.

43

Indignant then, 'twas Walter's turn to gripe:
"Excuse me! Mark it zero, as is right,
And as was written in the rules we know
And all agreed to 'fore we 'greed to throw.
Your foot was over Smokey, that's quite plain.
As punishment you've zero for this frame.
I say this not to be arbitrar'ly cruel:
This isn't 'Nam. It's bowling. There are rules."
The Dude and conflict never were fast friends;
He interceded then to make amends:
"Hey Walter, man. I beg you; please lay off.
It's obvious that he meant well enough.
Consider who your foe is 'ere you fight;
D' you really want to spar with Smokey t'night?
Fuck! So his toe slipped o'er a bit this frame.
Just let it go, man. This is just a game!"
But Walter, unconvinced, just turned his head
And shook it in confoundment as he said,
"It's 'just a game'? No, Dude. I must object.
This is a league game 'f I recall correct.
This game determines who advances on;
The tourn'ment's next round robin's fate is drawn.
It's more than just a game, Dude. Am I wrong?"
"Yeah but..." protested Smoke, who was cut off

As "Am I wrong?" pushed Walt through righteous scoffs.
So Smokey carried on, "Yeah but, just wait.
I wasn't o'er the line, at any rate.
Give me the marker, Dude. I'm markin' it eight."
With those words Smokey ambled to the desk;
He gained the pen with no more need to ask,
Then bent to mark the score that he thought just.
By that point Walt saw red and tasted rust.
Walt reached between his knees into his bag;
Then he produced a lump hid in a rag.
The rag, removed, revealed he'd drawn a gun.
He calmly spoke, though 's mind had come undone:
"My friend, dear Smokey, let me make this plain;
You mark it eight, you're in a world of pain."
At that the din in th' alley was downplayed
As Donny slowly slid downbench away.
"A world of pain," then Walter did repeat
Despite The Dude's protests and Smokey's bleat.
At sight of Walter's weapon, Smoke recoiled,
His hands up at his shoulders; he'd been foiled.
"I'm not..." he started to concede defeat
But "world of pain" was Walt quick to repeat.
"Look," Smokey quaked, "Dude, this man is your friend."
With hopes that sympathy'd cause this to end.

The Dude had no more want for this t' resume
Than Smokey did, and reasonably presumed:
"Now Walter, put the piece away and stop.
I'm warning you; they're calling up the cops."
But Walt with rage just twisted 'round his neck
And, standing, started screaming as he spake:
"My mind must surely warp the words I hear
For naught but mad men's concepts grace my ears.
Your tongues defy all logic, as would fools'.
Does no one give a shit about the rules?
I'll not abide a cheater on this day,
So mark it zero Smokey, 'nd walk away."
All sounds were off by then save for the yaps
Of Cynthia's dog whose leaps reached Walt's kneecaps.
The Dude and Smokey hesitated then
While "Mark it zero!" Walter screamed again.
He cocked his gun and with a marksman's grace
He aimed point blank at Smokey's ashen face.
Held hostage now, and frozen to the floor,
The Dude and Smokey prayed there'd be no more.
With measured subtlety The Dude leaned in
To grippen Smokey's hand around the pen
Then dragged his arm down to the scorer's plate
Where Smokey drew a zero (not an eight).

When friendships last friends see each other true;
Right then The Dude viewed Walter all anew.
Now Smokey'd finished up, the marker loosed,
He backed away from Walter, looked abused,
And slowly low'red his arms down as he cried,
"What mean a reason to have almost died!
Behold! Your precious score has been maintained!
Your glorious next round robin's been attained!
It's fucking zero, Walter, 's you decree,
And all you had to do was threaten me.
You persecute the world for going mad,
But if you're not much worse you're just as bad.
You win! Big deal! I guess you've all the luck!
I hope you're happy now, you crazy fuck."
Appeased then, Walter sat back on his seat.
His piece returned to th' bag between his feet.
With forcéd nonchalance and with no shame
He half apologized: "It's a league game."

In moments Dude and Walter'd left that place
And through the parking lot their steps retraced.
Each bowler lugged his ball to Duder's car
While Walter also had the carrier
(Its contents, though, were not cooped up inside;

As both men walked the dog pranced on behind).
While they walked on The Dude discussed the night:
"Walter, my friend, you're too gung-ho to fight.
You cannot carry on 's if life were war;
Those guys, like me, are peaceful to their core.
They're pacifists and Smokey dodged Vietnam.
He objected conscientiously at the time."
The mood of Walt was as if nothing'd passed
That should have made his heart beat twice as fast.
He said, "You know, Dude, I myself 've endorsed
Your pacifism. Though not in 'Nam, of course."
Unfazed by that retort The Dude pressed on:
"Your outburst on the lanes was outright wrong.
A guy like Smokey shouldn't face your gat;
The man has problems, emotional ones at that!
(Between Dude's words, with sarcasm Walt spat:
"You mean beyond this pacifism scat?")
He's fragile, man! He's quite a fragile guy;
He almost wept when you made him comply."
With that The Dude had ducked into his ride
While Walt packed dog and gear in th' other side.
"I did not know that," Walt said, truly taught
's he deftly slammed the rear side car door shut.
He sat beside The Dude 'n the passenger seat

As cop cars squealed behind them from the street.
The Dude and Walter watched as coppers tore
Into the lot then into th' alley's door.
Said Walt: "Oh well. It's water under th' bridge.
Now we advance to a rank with more prestige.
By hook or crook tonight we won the day,
And live anew next round to further play.
Our dispatched foes shouldn't bother you a ton;
We enter the next round robin. Am I wrong?"
"You aren't wrong," The Dude was 'bout to explain
But "Am I wrong" again was Walt's refrain.
"You aren't wrong," said Dude 's he turned his key,
"You're just an asshole," he added angrily.
The Dude had turned to face his friend, but Walt
Looked straight ahead, all casual, not at fault.
"All right then," Walter shrugged, and then went on,
"Next week our foes are O'Brien and Quintana.
They should be pushovers, Dude, so fear not,"
But Walt's bravado Dude had not quite bought.
At times it could be hard to hold so dear
A friend like Walt who was so cavalier.
"Just take it easy, man," The Dude then breathed,
And pushed down with his hands 'n a gentle heave.
They sat there in the car, sat in the lot,

And this time 'twas Dude's poise Walt hadn't bought.
Walt said, "Y' know Dude, that's been your reply
To everything that's passed 'tween you and I.
'f I took it easy every time we quarreled,
Light as a breeze without a care in the world,
I wouldn't be the man I am today:
A fit, robust American; proud to say.
And also I'll say this, my peaceful friend:
Your pacifism's not the living end.
Regard our situation, my comeback,
Involv'ng that camel-fucker in Iraq.
Your pacifism is a hollow more.
Your life may be a breeze, but bowling's war."
The Dude, not getting through, renewed his tack:
Just take it easy, man!" he volleyed back.
But Walt just straightened his shirt with light aplomb,
"On th' contrary, Dude, I'm perfectly fucking calm."
The Dude, instead of driving, broke with sound,
"Yeah, calm like waving a fucking gun around?!"
He said with so much vigor he nearly spit
While Walter coyly played the opposite:
"Calmer than you are, Dude," he quickly claimed
As if that statement won some kind of game.
"Just take it easy, Walter," Dude let on

(It pissed him off that Walt was playing calm).
But Walt once more, to seal his triumph tight,
Said, "Calmer than you are," a second time that night.
He wouldn't meet Dude's gaze but listened he
For Dude's response, but it never came to be.

That night with Walter all dropped off at home,
The Dude was glad to have some time alone.
A gorgeous Persian rug lie on his floor
Contrasting with his furniture so poor.
He'd donned his favorite robe of purplish pink
And hovered at the bar to mix a drink.
Kahlua, vodka, milk and ice he stirred;
White Russians were the cocktail he preferred.
Above the bar a photo neatly hung
Showed Richard Nixon in a bowler's lunge.
The Dude glanced at it; chuckled as he poured,
While th' answering machine played th' tape it stored:
"Hey Dude, it's Smokey. Guess you aren't in.
I called before; I thought I'd try again.
So look. There's one thing I don't want to be
And that's a hard-on 'bout this thing, you see?
I know it's not your fault, Dude, by the way,
But your man Walt was out of line today.

Well anyway, I just thought you should know
That Gene and I cannot just let this go.
Our next step is t' submit this to the league,
(I know this news endows you with fatigue)
And maybe see 'f they'll set aside the round
Or forfeit it to us if they're so bound.
But like I said, you know, fair warning, Dude.
I'm sorry, man. Tell Walter for me, too."
Just when The Dude thought life had evened out
This episode cast all of it into doubt.
The answering machine called out its beep
And played another message from its keep:
"Mr. Lebowski, hello. This is Brandt.
I'm call'ng from Mr. L'bowski's. How 'bout that?
A wonderful coincidence! Sublime!
Please call us at the earliest convenient time."
The Dude was not surprised that Brandt had called.
He'd been treading on his boss's rug, aft'r all.
Dude'd no intent to call that square-head back;
He let the answering machine play its next track:
"Mr. Lebowski, Fred Dyanarski here,
On b'half of the So-Cal Bowling League, I fear.
I've just received an informal report;
A man on your team has dishonored the sport.

It violates league rules, needless to say,
To draw a firearm amidst league play..."
The message carried on as Dude just hung
T' admire the rug; that's when the doorbell rung.
With drink in hand he opened up his door
And there stood Marty, all of 5'4".
The Dude, relaxed, leaned up against the jamb
And toasted slightly, "Marty. How are ya, man?"
From three steps down the height of Marty lacked;
His head reached to the waist of Duder's slacks.
All bald and husky, shorts and black socks-clad,
This Marty seemed a cherub (or one's dad).
What news he brought! Excited as he was,
His hands were fists, his voice a trembly buzz,
"Oh, Dude!" he smiled, "What I have to tell you!
I finally booked the space I wanted to.
It's there where I'll perform my dance quintet –
You know, my cycles – my best achievement yet.
Crane Jackson's Fount'n Street Theater, Tuesday night.
I've this request, Dude, take it as you might:
I'd love you to come down, 'f I may promote,
Then hang around and maybe give me notes."
He said this plaintively and bowed his head.
The Dude sipped his White Russian as he said,

53

"Okay, I'll be there, Marty," unabashed
And restful as he sucked his milk mustache.
Dismissed then, Marty grinned and turned to go,
But realized he'd one more thing Dude should know.
"Uh, Dude?" he quaked, almost ashamed to speak,
"Tomorrow's already the tenth, this coming week."
"Far out," Dude swallowed, glad to hear the news.
Poor Marty wasn't willing t' press issues
But Dude had missed his point so with a glance
Did Marty give The Dude a second chance.
A moment passed and Dude just stood there, dumb.
Then he caught on, and sipped, and clicked his tongue.
"Oh, okay, man," Dude nodded, now aware.
Of th' second reason Marty'd shown up there.
"Just slip the rent check underneath my door,"
Said Marty, finishing this task deplored.
The Dude said he'd comply and Marty left,
His eagerness a poor match for his heft.
The Duder closed the door and went inside
Where th' league official's message onward played:
"...A serious infraction, y'understand?
't the very least you'll draw a reprimand.
(At worst your partner Walter could be banned)."
The message ended and The Dude exhaled

Determined not to let his highness fail.
Just then it seems an angel must have sang.
Dude smirked, inspired, and into dance he sprang.
A slow tai chi: he'd melt from move to move,
Atop his rich new rug he found his groove.
A beep, and then the answering machine
Sung out once more; its final balladeen:
"Mr. Lebowski, this is Brandt again.
Please do give us a call when you get in.
And let me just assuage you," said he, smug,
"You needn't avoid this call 'cause of the rug,
Which I assure you, Dude, in any case
Is not the present problem with which we're faced.
We need your help with something's just come in
And, well ... we'd like you to stop by again.
I've carried on. I'm sorry. Pard'n my rant.
Please call us. Anytime, Dude. This is Brandt."
The Dude kept moving as the message played.
He posed as cranes and dragons, hands all splayed.
His interest piqued, his hand first then his head
Brushed toward the d'vice's table where it laid.
Without the will to put more garments on,
He chugged, and rolled a joint, and then was gone.

Inside Lebowski's home all lights were dimmed.
All with morose endampment was it brimmed.
A dolorous soprano sang inside;
She echoed off the hallways' walls, then died.
All ornaments which glimmered once were dull,
The angels which had hugged them, in a lull,
Refused to dance about the place's floors;
A sadness hung on all its heavy doors.
When Dude arrived Brandt met him at the gate;
He hurried him as if both men were late.
The Dude, three steps behind, matched Brandt's swift pace
(Though stonéd as he was, he wouldn't race).
Their footsteps echoed down the marble tile,
While Brandt a'jabbered on, one minute per mile:
"We've had the worst news one could ever bring;
Mr. Lebowski, sad and 'fraid, poor thing,
Is in seclusion in the western wing."
At end of hall a double door was found
Which Brandt shoved op'n with thunderous resound.
The aria which played throughout the lair
Grew louder now, its origin laid bare:
A private study, dark as a spent pyre
Save for the light from fireplace's fire.
Then Brandt, with choreography well-planned,

Leaned back against the jamb and raised a hand.
Head bowed, he pointed into dimméd room;
He dared not turn his gaze into that tomb.
"Mr. Lebowski," 'nnounced he. 'Twasn't clear
Which man he meant t' announce could be found here.
Regardless, sauntering, The Dude went in.
His host, before the fire, amid the din,
With blankets was all swaddled 'round his lap,
Sat looking at the flames as if to nap.
Behind him Duder crossed and took a seat
Atop a desk with gilded nouveau feet.
Not looking up, his focus ne'er to break,
And trembling in voice, Lebowski spake:
"It's funny, yes, though somberly I sit.
I think of life and what I've made of it.
I can look back upon a string of foes
Who've fallen at my feet and kissed my toes.
Competitors I've known all fell away
To make me this achievéd man today.
The obstacles I've overcome were great
But trample them I did at any rate.
Most men accomplish things, but I've done more
And all without my legs atop the floor.
What makes a man, Lebowski? Tell me that."

"Dude," Dude corrected, as pot seed he spat.
Lebowski asked again, his voice all low.
The grinning Dude just shrugged, "Sir, I don't know."
"Is it," Lebowski offered, "being prepared
To do the right thing, though the cost's unfair?
Isn't that what makes a man, a man?"
He asked, the fire flick'ring at his pain.
The Dude, all buzzed and contemplative then,
Said, "That and a pair of testicles, my friend."
Annoyed, Lebowski, taking nothing light,
Said thus: "You're joking, but perhaps you're right."
So far the mood was as if someone died
But Dude, our hero, took it all in stride.
For instance, Dude picked out that moment t' say,
"Excuse me, do you mind 'f I do a jay?"
From his shirt pocket he produced a spliff
And wet it once with a pass across his lips.
Without permission then he lit his joint;
Lebowski then said, "Bunny..." with no point.
"Excuse me?" Dude exhaled 'long with his smoke
And waited for an answer as he toked.
The firelight glowed orange on both men:
Lebowski's face showed tear tracks, hid till then.
"Bunny Lebowski," said he, "My loved wife.

Charm of my existence! Light 'f my life!
Today she's blindly wrought my worst of fears.
Are you surprised then, sir, to see my tears?"
The Dude, who'd just inhaled, set out to say
A mouthful, only managed "Fucking A."
Lebowski, wracked with sorrow, then replied,
His voice a'wavered, "Strong men also cry."
Then feebler still said, "Strong men also cry."
The Dude, high as he was, saw what this bode
And joint in hand, he switched to focus mode.
And just in time, Lebowski raised a hand
To signal out an order to his man.
"I received a fax this morning," he bemoaned.
As Brandt produced the fax, his boss intoned:
"Look ye upon this fax and mark its words.
Its letters tear my heart as they were swords.
As you can see, it is a ransom note
Sent here by cow'rdly men, I have no doubt.
A gang of wimps unable to achieve
On playing fields where higher mortals cleave.
Anon'mous curs who wouldn't sign their names
And forego effort 'n the name of deadly games.
They're scavengers who feed on real men's crumbs.
Not worth a nickel. Weaklings. Cowards. Bums."

The missive Brandt had handed to The Dude
Was thrown together all concise and crude,
Composed of clipped-out letters, grossly glued:
"We have your wife; ask not where she is hid.
Suffice to say you'll do just as we bid.
Go gather you one million dollars hence
In unmarked non-consecutives, all twent's.
Your wife we have the power now to snuff;
Await instructions, sir. No funny stuff."
The flimsy sheet flopped over in his hands,
The Dude once more reviewed the dire demands
Then, "Bummer," said he, "That's a bummer, man."
"You steel yourself for our proposed travails
And Brandt will fill you in on the details,"
Was all Lebowski said, chin in his palm,
So somber and so sad, yet almost calm.
With tugs The Dude was led away again
By Brandt towards the hallway whence they came.
The Dude looked o'er his shoulder at his host
Glow'ng orange in the firelight like a ghost.
Reserved he sat there thinking in his chair
Just motionless, as if he'd not a care.

The door behind them shut, the opera hushed,

They parked inside the hallway where they'd pushed.
Then Brandt, all solemn, turned around The Dude
To speak in whispers as he had been cued:
"Now Dude, my boss, a man of well-known means,
Has let me know he'll deal with all these fiends.
He is prepared to offer you a sum,
A generous amount, no paltry crumb,
To act as courier in the event
That their instructions they deign to present."
Such was his grim concern Brandt pumped his hand
Before his chest t' make sure his words'd land.
"Why me, man?" asked The Dude, whose point was fair.
Why'd he be hired to aide the millionaire?
Had he not just before been broadly scorned
By th' man whose rug Dude's pad was now adorned?
So Brandt explained to Dude, "My boss suspects
A point exists 'ere your life and his connect.
The very men who hid away his light
May be the thugs who ... soiled ... your rug that night.
Of course, the rug being yours you'd be well-learned
To see his guess confirmed or disconfirmed."
"He thinks the carpet-pissers did this, though?"
T'which Brandt replied, "Well Dude, we just don't know."

CHAPTER V

Then later on that night, back at the lanes
The gang had come to roll some practice frames.
'n an adjacent lane there stood a snakelike man,
Long fingernails and rings on both his hands,
His ponytail from 'neath his hairnet hung.
Raised bowling ball; he licked it with his tongue.
Prepared to bowl, the Spaniard full of grace
Approached as Spanish strings rang through the place.
An Eagles cover with some Latin flare
Conveniently played out, so debonair.
In purple coverall for pant and vest,
With satin sheen, and "Jesus" on his chest,

He let one fly, its aim completely true;

Ten pins were struck, and all ten of them flew.

With no surprise at all he turned to face

His partner (who an "X" had long since traced).

Then Jesus low'red his bod in a courtly bow,

He and his partner pointed, all for show.

No sooner then the song sped to its stride,

Did Jesus dance a Capoeira glide.

All this was watched by Walter and The Dude.

Back at their desk, heads cocked, they sat and stewed.

"Fucking Quintana," said The Dude with ire,

"That creep can roll," he started to perspire.

With worriedness was this concession leaked

For he and Walter faced Jesus next week.

"That may be true," said Walt, "but he's a perv."

The Dude agreed without moving a nerve

And not so much at what his words had meant,

But just t' agree with Walt's maligned intent.

"I mean it," Walt popped, "Yeah, it's all quite true.

He went to jail for doing what pervs do.

A sex offender with a record, he

Touched 'n eight year-old and went to Chino, see?"

As Walt explained why Jesus'd seen those walls

Quintana and his partner cleaned their balls.

The corners of a towel each had gripped
And back and forth in each their pounders slipped.
Accord'ng to Walt when Jesus was set free
He ended up in Venice perm'nently
Where he was made to walk from door to door
And tell each neighbor 'bout his crimes d'amor.
"Imagine every house until block's last;
You say hello, and you're a pederast."
"A pederast? What's that?" asked Donny then,
Abruptly interrupting Walt again.
So, "Shut the fuck up, Donny," Walter sighed
So used to him now it was took in stride.
Walt's interest in Jesus then was spent;
He spun his head to Dude to reconvent:
"How much they off'r you, anyway?" he asked.
"Some twenty-thousand bucks!" The Dude smiled back,
"Of course, as well, I get to keep the rug.
That I had taken it didn't seem to bug."
Walt grinned, "All this for handing off some cash?"
He beamed, daydreamed, and scratched at his mustache.
"That's right," Dude said, "I got a beeper, too.
In case they need me, they'll know what to do."
At once concern washed over Walter's face:
"What if it's dur'ng a game, this call they'll place?"

The Dude put Walt at ease: "I told them, 'Hey,
If you guys page me while we're in league play..."
"If what's in league play?" Donny butted in.
At th' interjection Walter's rant'd begin:
"For your convenience life's not made to fit,
Nor stop for you, you mis'rable piece of shit."
"What's wrong with Walter, Dude?" hurt Donny asked.
The Dude thought this rhetorical. It passed.
"I see no harm in being involved in this;
Odds are the girl kidnapped herself, I guess."
All this Dude said and thus he sealed his fate.
How could he 've known that Walter'd be irate?
What sea of woes is stirred with righteous pride?
Walt's interest piqued, The Dude's visage he eyed.
To clear up Walter's "huh?" then Donny puzzed,
"What do you mean, Dude?" in short breaths he buzzed.
The Dude held court as a professor would;
He gestured with his hands t' be understood:
"Rug pee'rs didn't pull this caper, man.
Consider all the points we know offhand:
Young trophy wife, if I may use the term,
Marries for wealth so that she needn't earn.
But, ah! To her dismay she seems to find
Her hubbie's purse-strings hardly e'er unwind.

What's more she owes more money than the Fed

To every Jackie, Johnny, Jim, and Ted.

("That ... fucking ... bitch!" with venom Walter spewed)

He'd see it's all a fake if he'd be shrewd.

It's all like Lenin said; you look for he

Who benefits to figure out, to see,

You know, who will, you know what I mean to say ..."

The Dude was stuck but Donny'd save the day:

"I am the Walrus," offered he, blasé.

Again did Walter make his anger known:

"That fucking bitch!" he fervently intoned.

The Dude's point made, he nodded to agree

(Again, then Donny jogged Dude's memory;

"I am the Walrus," called he helpfully).

So Walt howled, "SHUT THE FUCK UP DONNY! Fuck!

'Twas V. I. Lenin's quote that Dude had stuck!

It's Vladimir Ilyich Uly'nov said the phrase,

And here you quote The Beatles in a daze!"

Then Donny shrank, defensive as he asked,

"The fuck's he talking about?" through anguished mask.

As usual this query went unheard,

Or 't least unanswered as the rest conferred.

With dour resolve then Walt took up the fight:

"Of course that's what went on, Dude. Yes, you're right.

Oh man, you know, that makes me fucking sick."
He stressed the last word with a bod'ly flick.
The Dude, still Zenlike, asked why Walter cared
And Donny asked, "Yeah, Dude. What's with Walt's glare?"
Now it was Walter's turn to put on airs.
To make his point he squared his Brunswick'd feet
And slid his mass to th' edge of plastic seat:
"Those fucks! Those rich and wealthy holes of ass!
Shit, this whole fucking thing's devoid of class.
I didn't go to 'Nam and watch friends die
Face-down in muck that reached but inches high
So that this whore, this strumpet, bawdy tart..."
But Duder cut him off 'ere he could start:
"I wish you'd rein it in and just be calm;
This has nothing to do with Vietnam."
So Walter, interrupted, status slipped,
Put logic, as he knew it, on his lips:
"The link exists, let's not throw up a fence;
If nothing else it's literal in sense..."
Frustration made The Dude close both his eyes
"There isn't a connection," he replied,
"Your roll," he told his friend to move things on.
"Fine, have it your way," Walt said, that point gone.
"The point of this," he said, to save some face.

"Your roll," said Dude, to put him in his place.
And so The Dude and Walter traded quips
With "your roll" and "my point is" on their lips.
Until a voice called them, with accent struck:
"I hope you two are ready to be fucked!"
The Dude and Walter halted their debate
And looked up at the man who dared berate.
'Twas Jesus in his jumpsuit, smiling wide
There with his partner, beaming out with pride.
On his way out, he held his satchel bag;
From th' lip of lanes he carried on his brag:
"I hear you gringos rolled a decent game,
And found the semi's on your road to fame.
Oh, dios mio! Me and Liam here,
Are gonna fuck you up this weekend, hear?"
The Dude then conjured th' best insult he can:
"Oh yeah, well, that's like just y'r opinion, man."
Quintana took a step and stood up tall,
Addressing Walter in his Baja drawl:
"And let me tell you something, pendejo,
Your history and your crazy shit we know.
You pull that shit out there up on the lanes,
You pull your piece and seek to blow our brains,
I'll take your gun from you with moves so quick,

I'll stick it up your ass all pasty thick,
Then pull the trigger till the gun goes click."
Dumbfounded by this litany handed down,
In vain The Dude said, "Jesus" through his frown.
"You said it," Jesus beamed, glad he'd been named,
"Nobody fucks with th' Jesus," he refrained.
He left the lanes with Liam just behind
As Dude and Walter, seated, paid them mind.
With furrowed brow The Dude watched Jesus leave
And Walt said, "Eight year-olds, Dude," o'er his sleeve.

At home that night The Dude smoked till he w's gone;
He lay on his new rug with headphones on.
Instead of music playing there within,
The Venice Beach League Playoffs' clattering pins
Resounded in his headset as he dozed,
A smile on his face and both eyes closed.
The angels danced around his head in rings,
Sang th' journey of a bowling ball as it sings.
Just as the pins were scattered on his tape
The Dude's eyes opened upward 'ere he gaped.
Above him stood a woman red of head;
On each side stood her stooges, denim-clad.
At this intrusion, Dude could only gasp

For in a hurry, quicker than an asp,

Redhead looked right and that man swung a sap

That struck The Duder's jaw with such a clap

His head snapped down and slammed against the rug

While the angels danced his pain and flashbacked drugs.

Then all at once a million stars were scattered in the black.

The strains of Dylan's "Man In Me" came slowly playing back.

In blackness then the rug was floating up above L.A.

At twilight off it undulated as it flew away.

The Dude, awake, found himself flying, swimming through the sky,

A floating impulse in his chest, a twinkle in his eye.

He looked ahead to see the rug as it flew just as well

With redhead seated like a sheik upon it as it sailed.

In bill'wing shirt The Dude tried out a lazy swimming stroke.

The rug departed quickly, though, as slowly there he poked.

He closed the distance slightly but he couldn't understand

How this bowling ball had found its way into his forward hand.

The smile on his face became a look of deep concern.

Then physics made some sense again and down his arm was turned.

The tug of gravity had ceased his nice transcendent flight

And Earthbound to L.A. he plunged with wails and screams of fright.

Before he landed blackness once again was all around.

All through the air The Dude could hear a distant thund'rous sound.

The darkness, it turned out, was the inside 'f a ball return;

A giant one, and Dude was stranded up on it, he learned.

Then like a force of nature, from the maw of the device,

A bowling ball all black and tall was rolling into place.

The Dude, in state all shrunken, standing in that mammoth's way,

In terror was he frozen, w'out the nerve to run away.

So o'er and o'er the ball approached to flatten out The Dude.

His fate was sealed unless, by chance, a hole rolled where he stood.

He squared his slouchéd shoulders and he made himself go thin,

And, just his luck, the thumb-hole overtook him; he went in.

Before he knew the darkness of that hole gave way to light;

A bowler had picked up the ball and sent it into flight.

From out the hole The Dude could see who'd made the giant play;

The redhead, now a titan, followed through 's he rolled away.

In quick succession then he saw the lights, the pins, the floor,

With every roll the redhead giantess receded more.

And with the ominous forbearance of a gath'ring storm

The pins grew closer every roll, and each revealed its form.

Before too long the ball had struck the pins with such a smack

That chaos overwrote it all, and all went back to black.

Then back on Earth The Dude awoke in pain
With throbbing in his jaw and in his brain.
When dreams can let a man fly past his woes,
What misery is found in earthly throes!
The Dude reached up and prodded at his lip;
"Oh shit," he said 'n a groan that he let slip.
His headphones from his ears had been abashed;
A table lay upended, contents smashed.
His beeper beeped and beeped with no escape.
Its sound drowned out the bowling on Dude's tape.
From all this noise, no sense The Dude could wring
(To top it off the phone began to ring).
They'd broken in, they'd dealt his face a slug,
But worst of all they stole the fucking rug.

The beeper and the phone had both been Brandt.
Dude donned a bowling shirt and loose sweatpants.
He grabbed his shades and just before he'd roll
He found a roach and packed it in a bowl.

The Big Lebowski's house was dark again;
That aria sang out the mansion's pain.
The Dude and Brandt walked down a narrow hall
And Brandt was acting late so they'd not stall.
Brandt checked his watch to get his story straight:
"The culprits called the house at half-past eight.
Since then there've passed some eighty minutes hence.
They left you clear instructions 'n th'incidence.
They want you to go north on 405.
You'll have the money with you as you drive.
In forty minutes they will call a phone
That's portable, that we'll provide on loan.
One person only, or I'd go with you;
About that point they'd hear no different view.
(If it weren't thus I'd ride there with you, too.)
Our time is short; we mustn't hem and haw.
Oh, by the way, what happened to your jaw?"
Among the gold-laced hallway's art did stand
A Viking bust with trident in her hand;
They'd reached a desk outside Lebowski's den.
"Oh, nothing, uh, don't worry 'bout it, man,"
The Dude replied while cradling his jaw
As Brandt unlocked the desk's big filing drawer.
He reached inside and pulled two cases out:

An attaché and a cell phone half as stout.
"Well, here's the money and the phone you'll need.
Whate'er instructions they give, I beg, take heed.
Her life is in your hands," Brandt told The Dude,
The seriousness of which, some shock imbued.
"Don't say that, man," said Dude, whose buzz shook loose,
But Brandt was resolute with this abuse:
"I've been asked to repeat that so you'll know;
Her life is in your hands, Dude. Hurry; go!"
The Dude, then worried, begged futile demands
So Brandt replayed, "Her life is in your hands.
Report to us as soon as it is done."
And Brandt walked off as primly as a nun.
The Dude, with hands all full, watched Brandt walk out;
He'd thought this Bunny safe but now had doubt.
Suppose she had been kidnapped as they'd said?
What slight misstep from he could find her dead?

With that The Dude drove off but made a stop
To pick up Walt at th' Army Surplus shop.
Sobchack Security was all locked down;
Its owner stood out front behind a frown.
As Dude pulled in Walt headed for the car.
At driver's side he opened up Dude's door.

In 's right hand was a satchel, and in left
A bulky paper bundle did he heft.
"Move over, Dude, and grab the ringer quick,"
Did Walt command 's he slid behind the stick.
The Dude, confused, slid over as was told
And asked his friend what he'd asked him to hold.
"The ringer!" Walt responded, clear as day
As if this should have been known right away.
They barreled down the road into the night,
Walt dressed in camo shorts, his headband tight.
The Dude examined what this ringer held;
Some dirty underwear and socks that smelled.
He pawed through these contents, was just bemused,
"The hell is this?" he half-asked, half-accused.
"My dirty undies. Laundry, Dude. The whites,"
Was Walt's reply, tongue half-out in delight.
With mean disgust Dude brusquely dropped the bag
And realized bringing Walt would be a drag.
As side streets then to highway gave their way,
Dude gave his friend a chance to have his say:
"Dear Walter, I implore you, tell me why'd
You bring your underwear to meet these guys?"
There is a type of man who'll not reveal
The workings in his mind and, like a heel,

He'll hoard his every thought and make it known
Though each man has his thoughts, his are his own.
To get a clue from Walt was pulling teeth.
You'd have to ply him, it would seem, till death.
For instance t' answer Dude's last verbal jab
Walt cryptically responded, tonally drab:
"That's right, old friend, for this to go off well,
The ringer can't appear an empty shell.
The weight! The weight is why I brought the clothes.
They'll not suspect us once they must lift those."
The Dude, exasperated, lost for words,
Felt tension in his mind's load-bearing cords:
"But Walter, what the fuck caused you to think
We'd need these garments for this dire hijink?"
So Walter at the wheel, eyes on the road,
In storyteller's cadence did unload:
"Exactly, Dude. I did think; thought all night,
About this job, about our abject plight.
A measly fucking twenty grand's on th' line;
Why should we settle, thinking that'd be fine?"
Of what The Dude could barely make make sense,
One word especially caused dissonance:
"What 'we'? The fuck d' you mean when you say 'we'?
You sought to just ride 'long 's what you told me!"

Walt said, "My point is this, Dude; hear me through:
With all at stake will twenty thousand do?
We've got a million dollars in a bag,
Why settle when a fortune could be had?
Our troubles would be over before long.
My undies, or a million. Am I wrong?"
By now Dude saw what Walt had dared to dream;
A plot to steal that only Walt would scheme.
He said, "Yes Walt, you're wrong. I think you are.
It's not a fucking game we're playing here."
"Oh but it is a game!" Walt disagreed,
"You said yourself the woman's motive's greed.
Why should the fat-cats squander all their wealth?
Besides, as you said, she kidnapped herself."
The Dude could scoff as both men watched the road
But then the phone chirped its monot'nous ode.
The Dude and Walter turned their heads to look
At th' phone which Dude had taken off the hook.
With startled heart, receiver in his grip,
Dude pressed the green lit button by its clip.
He brought the phone to rest by his right ear
And, 's if at home, intoned the words, "Dude here."
It was so quiet then inside the car,
A German accent came in loud and clear:

"Who is this?" asked the voice on th' other end,
Confused, it seemed, by Dude's voice unconstrained.
And so Dude answered, cord hung 'cross his neck,
"It's Dude the bagman, man, who'd you expect?
You called the number for this phone and so
I answered it, now where d' you want us t' go?"
The Dude had said a mouthful 'bout his name
But one word in his speech was open game.
The German voice asked "Us?" and sounded terse;
He'd need The Dude to clarify his words.
The Dude, all mortified, realized his slip;
He was to ride alone on this road trip.
Dude low'red the phone to press it 'gainst his chest
And uttered "Shit!", his whispered voice depressed.
He looked at Walt and Walter looked at he,
Then he spoke in the phone 'gain, testily:
"Yeah man, you know. Me and the driver; 'us.'
I have him here and I'll explain that thus:
I'm not some octopus with several arms
That drive, hold money, quell the phone's alarms …
I'm not some Superman, no Beowulf,
I can't do all this by my fucking self."
"Just shut ze fuck up!" yelled the German then,
Which made The Dude's heart skip a beat again.

Both ends were silent after that command.
A moment passed. "Hello?" the voice began.
It'd been made clear that this call had gone wrong
So Walter interjected before long.
He yelled, "Dude, are you fucking this thing up?"
Loud 'nough to illustrate he'd blown his top.
The German must have heard all this commosh;
He asked, "Whose voice is this that dares encroach?"
The Dude, annoyed with Walter, stayed his tongue,
Then said, "The driver man." But up, they'd hung.
Dude blinked his eyes as dial tone played on;
He said, "Hello?" but realized they'd gone.
Confoundment turned to anger; Dude hissed, "Shit!"
They'd trusted him and Walter ruined it!
Still chafing, Walter bellowed at The Dude:
"The fuck is going on?" he asked all rude.
The Dude exploded, "Walt, I'm not your pup!
Don't chide me thus, 'twas you who fucked it up!
You fucked it up! Her life was in our hands!"
With such a force his veins stood out in bands.
Thus scolded Walter swallowed as he scowled,
Cocked for'rd his head as ever on they rolled,
And told his friend, "Be easy, let's not fret.
There's not a reason to get worked up yet."

He illustrated this by breathing in

While coolly pointing forward with his chin.

The Dude ignored this cooler-heads display;

He saw their spot in quite a different way:

"We're screwed now, Walter. Mark my words; we're screwed,

Or your name isn't Walt and I'm no Dude.

We don't get shit, no benefactor's cash,

And worse, they're gonna kill the girl, those trash!

Just like a flower from its garden plucked,

She'll die within some days. It's done. We're fucked."

He shook his head, a jitter on his neck,

And slammed the phone onto its charger deck.

His voice was coarse from screaming in dismay.

With no remorse, Walt lev'led his head to say,

"Nothing is fucked here, Dude. C'mon, relax.

You're being very un-Dude. They'll call us back.

You said yourself this kidnap plot was hers ..."

Abruptly then they heard the cell phone's noise.

"See, Dude?" said Walt in vindicated tones,

"I know my way 'round kidnappers and phones.

There's nothing fucked here, Dude. Just take my word.

Nothing is fucked; they're FUCKING amateurs."

This last bit Walter hollered with bombast

In case the kidnappers heard as th' phone passed.
(The 'Answer' button Dude had not yet mashed).
The Dude recoiled at that and made this known
Before he'd speak to Germans on the phone:
"Okay, Walter, just shut the fuck up, hear?
And don't say peep while I do business here."
He waited for agreement from his friend,
And, "Have it your way," Walt conceded t' end.
Thus satisfied, The Dude clicked on the set
But Walter wasn't finished speaking yet:
"But they're amateurs," he sotto vocé quipped,
For which The Dude shot him a glare, tight-lipped.
With open line and dead air taking time,
"Dude here," he greeted th' master of this crime.
The German spoke, all business, foul intent,
And said, "Okay. Vee proceed as vas meant.
But only if there is no funny stuff."
The Dude could hear no sign that this was bluff.
He just agreed, though all annoyed. And then
The German asked, "No funny stuff?" again.
Through with the way this labor'd seemed to slow,
"Just tell us where the fuck you want us t' go!"
With that this business was again unstopped;
The Germans gave directions to the drop.

The Dude and Walter drove on through the night.
But for a Creedence tape, 'twas mostly quiet.
L.A. gave way to desert as time passed
Where naught but brush and gravel had amassed.
The passing cars which had lit up their night
Gave up their posts to constant blue street lights.
'Fore long they passed a sign on highway's edge
Of two posts' width staked on the ditch's ledge.
The Simi Valley Road was what it marked;
"There goes the sign," Dude pointed as he barked.
He watched the sign recede with twist of waist,
Still pointing as it passed and 'round he faced.
With cigarette in lips Walt made them slow'r
And choked the wheel as two lanes shrank from four.
The silence broke, now Walter bolstered 's plan;
Momentously he pitched it to his man:
"All right, my friend, as long's we get her back,
Then no one's in a place to give us flack.
The girl restored at home in rel'tive peace;
He gets his wife, and we keep the baksheesh."
A bit astonished that this persevered,
Dude looked at Walt and petulantly sneered,
"That's fucking great, man, but I'll mention this:

You've not explained how we'll know where she is.
We keep the money locked tight in the pack,
But how does our deceit get Bunny back?"
'Twas all that Walt could do to stifle laughs;
He'd waited for that question for hours and halfs.
He smiled at Dude and smiled back at the road,
"That's th' simple part," he almost didn't explode,
"Immediately after we hand o'er the case,
I'll grab the guy and beat him 'round the face.
We'll rain down blows until he's overwhel'd,
And begging t' let him tell us where she's held!"
He let his plan sink in as best he could.
As plans went, Walter knew this one was good.
But Dude, still unimpressed, just rolled his eyes;
Sarcastically he rattled off some lies:
"Oh! What a plan! My, what a brain you've got!
That's fucking genius. Wish I'd had that thought!
No way this ruse could succumb to a botch.
So elegant! A Swiss-made fucking watch!"
With gleeful heart Walt basked in Duder's praise:
"That's right!" he sang, "I've had this plan for days.
The beauty of the thing's simplicity;
No danger we've missed some complexity.
For when a plan is overwrought and long

Things get fucked up and poorly thought and wrong.
If there's one thing I learned in Vietnam ..."
But then the phone rang out to break its calm.
Ignoring Walt, The Dude picked up the phone,
Half wishing he'd hear naught but dial tone.
He answered, "Dude," and said no more than that.
The static line buzzed as the German spat:
"Vee keep zis short to not keeps us on edge;
If you look north you'll notice vooden bridge.
When you cross bridge you'll srow bag high und far
From zee left window of zee moving car.
You're being vatched," then click, then dial tone.
The Dude said, "Fuck!" as he hung up the phone.
The sound of it made Walter jolt and balk
And ask, "What means the rudeness of your talk?
Did th' villain on th' line report where we should drive
T' exchange the cash for th' Big Lebowski's wife?"
Dude said, "The man confounds us in th' worst way;
The news is there is no hand-off, per sé.
At a wooden bridge whose distance is not far
We throw the money from the moving car."
This was bad news for Walt, who stared ahead;
His best laid plans, it seemed, had been laid dead.
His mouth agape, he tilted back his head:

"I'm sorry, Dude. We just can't do that, man.
A moving car? Nope. That fucks up our plan."
Said Dude, "Your plan is shot, my friend, that's all.
Unless you'd like to give those guys a call.
Yeah, call 'em back! That's how this thing'll work.
Explain how fucking simple 'tis, you jerk.
The beauty of the thing's simplicity.
Call back and lay it out explicitly."
The Dude had reached into the car's back place
And grabbed Lebowski's actual briefcase.
He held it in his lap with both his hands,
Determined then to not stray from their plans.
"A wooden bridge?" skulked Walter, scheming, mad,
Unable to allow the crooks t' be paid.
"We're throwing th' money man, not fucking 'round,"
The Dude admonished, head spinning 'n time with th' sound.
When men spring into action they're as trains
And onto track they've set their plotting brains.
No matter how much sense The Dude could make,
His man's quick plans would neither steer nor brake.
"All right," Walt said, "The bridge is coming up;
Hand me the ringer, Dude. Right now. Chop-chop!"
But Dude reached not for th' ringer at his feet;
Just grabbed the handle 'n his own Samsonite.

"Fuck that," Dude said, his plan set in as well,
"I love you, Walter, but I've got to tell
That soon (or not) you'll just have to admit
That you're a goddamn fucking idiot."
The bridge was then upon them; it was time.
The Dude sat up, but Walter blocked him in
By grabbing for the ringer on the floor
And rolling down the window 'n his own door.
"No time to argue Dude," Walt said in haste
's he pulled the ringer up to meet his waist.
"Here comes the bridge," he said with hand on wheel,
"And here the ringer goes!" he yelled with zeal.
And in a flash he gave his satchel flight;
End over end it spun into the night.
As Dude and Walter drove on off the bridge,
The undies-laden case soared o'er its edge.
'Twas chaos in the car once that had passed,
"Your wheel! I'm rolling out!" Walt ordered fast.
At the same time he flung his door ajar
While Dude, with left hand, harshly steered the car.
"What the fuck?" screamed Dude, all he could think;
The sudden gale had made him gag and blink.
"Your wheel!" repeated Walt with sergeant's clout,
"Stay fifteen em-pee-aitch. I'm rolling out!

I double back and grab him by the head
Then beat him till to Bunny's cell we're led.
The Uzi!" he requested, plain as days,
As if this small request was commonplace.
"What Uzi?" Duder stammered, head aspin.
(He'd lots more questions, but where to begin?)
His partner chuckled cruelly as he grabbed
The other package, taped and paper-wrapped.
Walt said, "You didn't think I'd take this trip
Without at least a sidearm in my grip?"
With moments not to spare did Duder plead,
"I beg you not to do this, Walt! Take heed!"
But Walt was ready leaning o'er the road;
In amped-up stance his c'mmando training showed:
"Fifteen! This's it! Now Dude, let's take that hill!"
And bellowing out to the road he spilled.
With Walter sudd'nly gone, Dude slid aside
Behind the wheel to straighten out his ride.
In frantic mind he swerved it down the street
Which just before had Walter dared to meet.
Walt hit the asphalt, grunted as he rolled,
And lost his Uzi, sliding into th' cold.
The paper-covered gun burst through its wrap
With bullets spray'ng, each a thunderclap.

This lethal spinning gun spat iron far;
At signposts, at the road, and at Dude's car.
A bullet flew into the left rear tire
And Dude had not been braced f'r its open fire.
Still fumbling his case, he lost control
And steered the car into a roadside pole.
Abruptly stopped, The Dude tossed for'rd and back
And blinked a sec to ponder the attack.
He'd all but given up; his cause was lost,
Till he remembered which case had been tossed.
What angel had reminded him his lot?
No matter. He picked up his case, dashed out,
And ran back down the road from which he'd crashed
To find his buddy Walter, knee all gashed,
Slow-limping tenderly back to the ditch,
To find the German 'neath his vooden britch.
Dude waved Lebowski's briefcase o'er his head;
He screamed, "We have it!" through his post-crash dread,
And caught up quickly to his injured friend
Whose sluggish double-back had met its end.
From under th' bridge an engine roared to life,
A headlight sliced the darkness like a knife,
A motorcycle bumped up from the creek,
It jolted, slowed, then turned after it peaked,

And as it sped away from Walt and Dude,
Two more escaping bikes could be construed.
As all their headlights vanished o'er a hill
The Dude and Walter stood hushed in the chill.
They stared a while as th' lights fishtailed away.
"Ah fuck it. Let's go bowling," 's all Walt'd say.

CHAPTER VI

And so it was, The Dude and Walt went back
On a spare tire the Dude had years hence packed
To their home lanes where alleys they could rent;
There's safety in one's home environment.
As Walter rolled The Dude just rode the pine.
Despondently he sat as his phone whined.
Ignoring that, he watched his partner bowl
Then take a seat to tally up his toll.
Dude wondered how his friend could be so cool
When just an hour prior he'd played the fool.
"Aitz chaim he," said Walter as he sat,
"The tree of life. My ex used to say that."

The Dude could no more hide his angered mind:
"The fuck's that s'pposed to mean?" he asked his friend,
"And furthermore, I hope you've written drafts
Of what we'll tell Lebowski when he asks."
It seemed that Walt sought only to keep score
As Dude's entreaty went all but ignored.
"What's that? Oh him," Walt dawningly realized,
"What exactly is the problem, in your eyes?"
The Dude expected so few things from Walt,
And none of them were his admitting fault,
But this time Dude could not believe his ear;
Did Walter not know what had happened here?
In starts and stops he 'xplained his point of view:
"What's the …? I mean … You were fucking there, weren't you?
I thought at least you'd demonstrate some fuss;
They'll kill that woman, all because of us!"
Now Walter glanced around up from his work,
His face with no concern, his ears no perk,
And asked "The fuck are you talking about now, Dude?
Now's not the time to cower like a prude,
For that poor woman (more like that poor slut)
Kidnapped herself to gain her husband's loot.
You said all this yourself, if I recall."

93

But calm's Walt was, Dude wasn't calmed at all:
"No Walt, I said I thought she did the deed,
But you're the one who thinks that's guaranteed.
You're certain 'bout a fact that I made up."
Walt nodded, "Absolutely certain. Yup."
He'd have gone on but then Donny arrived,
A trot 'n his step, a glimmer in his eyes.
He carried news he knew his friend would want:
"They've posted the next round of the tournament!"
So Walter, without thinking, spoke his mind:
"Hey Donny, shut the fuck ..." then re-aligned.
He turned from score to Donny for to say,
"What day have they determined when we'll play?"
Said Donny, "Saturday," his grin obtuse,
Obsequious, and glad to be of use.
At this was Walter cast into despair.
(Convenient that he'd now decide to care!)
"This Saturday?" he asked, then did the math,
"Oh no. They must re-schedule for my faith."
The Dude, ignored, could not care less about
The tournament or how it'd been laid out.
So, leaning in, he asked his friend again,
"Walt, what the fuck d' we tell Lebowski, man?"
But Walt, ignoring, or choosing to ignore,

Did not turn back to hear his friend implore;
Instead he conjured ire at this turn,
And found a worthy effigy to burn:
"I went to the league office, made some trips;
A thousand times the words have crossed my lips …
Pray tell me, Donny, what man, what mean scound'
Was put in charge of scheduling this round?"
The Dude begged Walt's attention yet anew,
But Donny gave the answer Walt was due:
"Burkhalter," he reported dutifully;
Then Walter summoned rage that bordered glee:
"I told that fucking kraut a thousand times
That I don't roll on Shabbas," Walter whined.
"It's already posted," Donny clarified.
"Well they can fucking unpost it!" Walt cried.
The Dude was made a cuckold to this speech,
But once more waded on into the breach:
"Hey Walter, man. Who gives a shit? It's moot.
The issue here's the money in my boot.
And what of this poor woman trapped in Hell?
When we approach Lebowski, what d' we tell?"
For Walt this trifle could go on for days;
He wouldn't let it grow him any grays.
"Come on," he said, still not quite facing Dude,

So's not to see his scowl of anguished brood,
"Eventually she'll tire of this game
And wander back from whence the harlot came."
The Dude could speak and wanted to at that,
But Donny asked a question 'fore he'd chat:
"Why is it, Walter, that on Saturdays
You do not bowl? You character it betrays!"
At this point Walter felt he could explode;
Through poor pretense of calm his tension showed.
He took a sec to calm his raging mind,
Before through gritted teeth, his yarn'd unwind:
"I'm Shomer Shabbas," said he, swallowing blood,
And chewing back his hate like so much cud.
"But what's that, Walter?" Donny asked, naïve,
Creating then a quiet that Dude'd relieve:
"Hey Walter, man, Judaica is swell;
Just help me think of something we can tell …"
At that point it came down to preference;
To edify Don or handle Dude's defense?
As hard a man as Walt himself professed,
He talked to Donny, letting Duder twist:
"Each Saturday is Shabbas, day of rest.
For modern Jews, a chance to reinvest,
To contemplate our faith and G-d's design,

And suffer nothing worldlily aligned.
On Shabbas I leave working off aside,
As cars I neither drive nor fucking ride,
I'll handle me no cash on Saturday,
Nor let the oven work its fiery way,
On Shabbas I cannot be made to bowl
Because I sure as shit DON'T FUCKING ROLL!"
This last rejoinder ended in a scream
That stood up Donny straight, his eyes abeam
And frightened up no words he'd dare unleash
Except a sanitized, unsharpened, "Sheesh."
"SHOMER SHABBAS!" Walter yelled again
(A kind of kosher yet incensed refrain).
Again The Dude leaned forward 's if to pray,
To glean from Walt what they should do or say.
He'd scarcely made the words but was shut down,
As "Shomer fucking Shabbas," Walter frowned.
The Dude could see now Walter didn't care
This much about what days to play were fair.
Instead he hemmed and hawed and yelled at Don,
Whom usually he'd rather see be gone.
What was this? Pride? Not knowing what to say?
Wherefore would Walter not meet Dude halfway?
No matter, thought The Dude as he gave in,

's he grabbed the phone and bag with ball therein
(Though "Fuck it" more would match the phrase he'd spin).
"I'm out of here," he then declared, and stood,
And stepped onto the carpet from the wood.
"Oh come on Dude, don't go away like that,"
Said Walter, though he didn't stand but sat.
He turned to Donny, sotto vocé said,
"Big fucking baby," as he cocked his head.
Hard-pressed would Donny be to disagree,
He just was glad that Walter'd spoke to he.
Alas, his stuff all grabbed then Walter rose.
He limped to follow Dude; their distance closed.
With bag in hand, the other hand midsleeve,
He spoke, and Donny followed 'ere they'd leave.
"Hey Dude, you know, just tell him what you will;
We made the handoff, no need to get shrill …"
"Oh, how'd that go?" then Donny asked anew,
Reminded only then 'f what they'd been through.
Said Walt, "All things considered, not too bad.
Though now Dude's car has more dings than it had."
At that report The Dude had spasms, cringed,
And doubled over as his mind unhinged:
"Please, Walter. Cease! Desist! I've heard enough!
You fool! There was no fucking cash handoff!

They didn't get their money after all!
They're gonna ... man, they're gonna ..." There he stalled.
Then Walter mocked his friend's afraid alarms
And swung, as a conductor, both his arms:
"Poor woman! Oh, they'll kill her! That poor lass!"
A few heads turned but most just let them pass.
The spectacle that Walter had put out
Was dim among the din and bowling routes.
To punctuate that point then Donny asked,
"If you don't drive, how d' you travel on Shabass?"
The question moot, to Duder Walter spake,
To emphasize for emphasis's sake:
"Dude, you surprise me. Those guys won't kill shit.
Nor do shit, Dude. Come on. I'm sure of it.
What can they do? They're fucking amateurs."
As he spoke on they crossed the alley's doors
And crossed into the nighttime parking lot.
"You're acting like they're pros but, Dude, they're not.
And anyway, look at the bottom line;
We've got the mil and what have they of mine?
My underwear! You see? My fucking whites!"
His voice cracked as he cackled in delight.
"And we've a million in our fucking car!"
"Our car?" asked Dude, who stopped and went not far.

Each man alike stopped with The Dude in place
And spied the sight 'f an empty parking space.
Walt's laughter shrank from high to low to gone;
Across his face reality broke dawn.
"Where is your car?" he asked (like "by the way…");
"Who has your undies?" Don caught up to say.
"Dude, where's your car?" Walt asked again with fright,
As if his words would haunt the very night.
For every spot within the lot was filled
But for the one where Dude's car had been wheeled.
"You mean you don't know?" sadly Duder asked;
His phrase was shards as o'er his tongue it passed.
"Well Dude," said Walter, shaken, still uneased,
"The spot you took was for the paralyzed.
Perhaps your car's been towed," Walt said, but knew
The last car from here towed was 'n '82.
"You fucking know it's stolen," Duder hissed,
As if some detail stood that Walt had missed.
They searched there for the car with all their might,
But not an angel remained. The Dude was right.
"The thought had crossed my mind," admitted Walt,
Who feared that somehow this was all his fault.
"Ah fuck it," said The Dude, but not resigned,
More like an angry fighter'd lost his wind;

Determined to press on another day,
But for the moment, being beat, just lay.
Upon his heel The Dude then turned and walked.
The phone slung from his shoulder lit and squawked.
So Donny asked, "Hey, where you going, Dude?"
"Donny, home," he answered, not t' be rude.
So Donny helped, "Your phone is ringing, Dude."
And "Thank you, Donny," came The Dude's reply
And home he walked to think, and then get high.

The Dude, once lifted, pulling all the stops,
Against his better judgment called the cops.
They showed and took a seat in the front room
Where angels 'stead of Duder's rug all loomed.
Cops took the couch, and Dude the La-Z-Boy.
The Dude was high but too proud to play coy.
Before their pow-wow hit its actual stride,
The cell phone ringed its ring and voices died.
It rang for minutes, never seemed to cease,
And th' cops were tense though Duder seemed at ease.
They watched each other wordlessly a while,
Surrounded by Dude's magazines in piles,
Amassed on tables set about the place,
Highlighted by this ashtray or that vase.

The ever-present magic 8-ball stood
Upon the central coffee table's wood
Aside an ashtray, flat and platter-sized,
That caught the gaze of th' veteran officer's eyes.
The couch the cops were on faced t'ward the door,
The younger one looked thirty, th' older more.
This rookie had his pen all poised to trap
Dude's words in th' notebook open in his lap.
The room was dim; two floor lamps lit it all.
They sat there darkly. No one took the call.
At last their caller seemed to call it quits
As rings gave way to silent, anxious fits.
A moment passed and not an angel coughed,
And Dude picked up about where he'd left off:
"A Gran Torino, Nineteen Sev'nty-Three."
The young cop wrote and asked Dude cordially,
"Could you tell us the color of the ride?"
"Yeah. Green with rust ... uh, coloration on th' side."
By then the older cop had found Dude's bowl;
A tiny bowling pin with two drilled holes.
He held it up, regarded all its sides,
And sniffed it with a face designed for chides.
The rookie cop asked, "What of value lay
Inside the auto stole from you today?"

The Dude knew he'd need to be cool as hash;
These cops did not need know about the cash.
"Huh? Oh yeah. Tape deck, and some Creedence tapes,
And then there was, you know, uh ... my briefcase."
He said it so mundanely, so blasé,
The cop just wrote the words, was on his way
To follow up that query, flush things out,
And (Dude suspected) find something to doubt:
"The briefcase, sir. Please, what were its contents?"
Dude here would need his coolness as defense
(Good thing he'd smoked not twenty minutes hence).
He reached down to his right, his hand knew where,
Pulled wooden lev'r and laid back in his chair.
"Just papers. You know, papers. Business sheets."
He rubbed his goatee, proud of his deceit.
"And what is it you do?" this rookie asked.
His interest piqued by th' squalor in which he basked.
"I'm unemployed," The Dude had to admit,
And for his home and clothes, none doubted it.
"My rug was also stolen," said The Dude,
Which caused the cops to look at him, heads skewed.
"The rug was in the car?" the rookie guessed;
It just seemed odd to share that detail last.
"No. Here," The Dude said, indicating 'round

With splayed hand sweeping, hov'ring o'er the ground.
As this went on Dude's landline rang its tones
(Though none from this crowd cared to answer phones).
"Oh, separate incidents?" guessed would-be Holmes.
As phone rang on, The Dude grew anxious, tense,
And tired of listing all his evidence.
"D' you find them often, when these cars get robbed?"
Still hopeful yet still nervous, timbre bobbed.
The rookie's bedside manner clicked on then,
"Sometimes," he offered, dulling some the pain,
"I must be honest though, for your own sake,
I wouldn't hold out hope for the tape deck …"
"The Creedence either," th' older partner gruffed
Between attempts to see if th' pipe was stuffed.
"And what about the briefcase?" Dude pressed on,
But shyly, spryly, no to be undone.
Before he further clarified his mean,
Dude's answering device began to screen:
"The Dude is not here; leave a message," then,
A woman's voice spoke on the other end,
"Mr. Lebowski? Can we meet? And when?
When you get home give me a call post haste;
I'll send a car for pickup to your place.
My name is Maude Lebowski. I'm no thug,

But I'm the woman who took back your rug."
The voice hung up. Dude turned to rookie, stunned.
"I guess we'll close the case on that," th' cop punned.

Just as Maude said, Dude called and was brought to
A loft on Rio Vista Avenue.
Where once a warehouse there had been just built,
Now artists worked their trades in homes ungilt.
A night had passed since Maude had called his phone;
In daylight now he walked into her home.
The midday sun shone through her entrance door,
Illuminating th' blackened concrete floor.
As Dude walked in his shadow shortened down
For all was dark and no one made a sound.
Throughout this loft which lay at th' end of th' hall,
All metal shelves and paintings hugged each wall.
Inside the dimméd lair, in th' air, but faint:
A singsong chant, the smell of new wet paint;
The Dude stopped halfway down to take a look
At splattered yellow on th' floor of the nook.
Fresh paint aground, The Dude looked in through squints
To spy a canvas, angled, bearing tints.
It stood there like a ramp in yonder room:
An angel painted in a splattered womb.

The image struck The Dude as artly mess,
Why it was propped like that was his to guess.
For who would leave a painting propped on blocks
Before a room where everybody walks?
The whispered singsong chanting drew e'er close
As Dude stood wond'ring at the angel's pose.
From o'er his head, behind him banged a sound
As if a rolling bowling ball hit ground.
It struck him odd as on the ball sang out,
Forever closer, turning him in doubt
To peer into the darkness 'ere it came
(He half-suspected God had bowled a frame).
Advancing on him, quicker than a flash,
An angel soared in harness and in sash,
But else all naked, thrashing, spinning arms,
The angel passed him, screeching her alarms.
He cowered as it happened, losing grace;
He raised his hand, but something caught his face.
Dude turned to watch her fly into the loft,
Receding nude, as stiff as she looked soft.
When o'er the painting down the hall she chugged,
She dropped some more of what had hit Dude's mug.
Dude realized, his fright becoming dim;
This angel was the artist who'd called him.

This painting at hall's end would be Maude's sign;
She had no wings, but pulleys and a line.
What lengths will artists fly to please their muse?
Their homes they'll mar, their bodies they'll abuse.
Her stroke, or (as it were) her splatter dropped,
She stilled her spinning arms and smoothly stopped.
The vision Dude took in then flushed his mind;
He watched the operation from behind:
Two men in leather shorts, with ropes in hand,
Pulled taut so Maude mid-air could rise to stand.
Surrounded as she was by art and mess,
Christlike she clashed, nude but for harness vest.
Stark furniture and paintings here were wed
(Grim portraits, prints, a scissors over red).
"I'll b' with you in a minute," came her sound
As, body like a cross, she floated down.
On land the men helped Maude out from her sling
As gently as they'd tug an angel's wing.
To man on left she passed her brushes off,
Then reaching b'hind her neck, her collar doffed.
Completely naked now in pale sunlight,
She turned t' her left and was robed from her right.
Her ritual complete, she turned to face
Her guest who walked to meet her at her pace.

Dumbfounded, Dude had not yet said a thing,
Preferring to let this red seraph sing:
"Mr. Lebowski, does the female form
Cause you discomfort well beyond the norm?"
She spoke with a commanding voice that filled
The cavernous apartment where they milled.
They walked toward each other till they'd stopped
Each at an end of th' painting, standing propped.
Dude asked, "Is that what's painted here?" and gazed
At newly splattered hues that dried and glazed.
Without a pause, without a moment's breath,
She answered Duder's question in some depth:
"It is, in one sense, just as you suspect:
My art has been commended (by who'd inspect)
As vaginal, and strongly so at that.
Which bothers men (just some, a pithy stat).
The word itself makes some men pale as pall.
Vagina." said she, punctuating all.
The flustered Dude, green specks upon his brow,
Asked, "Oh yeah?" plain as circumstances'd allow.
Maude answered, "Yes, they don't like hearing it
And, pressed to say it, stutter like some twit.
Whereas, without the bat of an eyelash,
He will refer in tones all unabashed

To his own 'dick', or 'rod', or 'johnson', e'en."
(That last gem took a sec for her to glean).
So, "Johnson?" asked The Dude to get it clear
How th' conversation'd made its way to here.
With nary a "hello", all pale and smug,
She talked a lot, but not about Dude's rug.
"All right, Mr. Lebowski, let's get down
To cases," said she as she turned around
To walk from hallway back into her place
While Dude, though shambling, tailed her at her pace.
Her loft was huge and, varied as it seemed,
A system ordered objects 'ere they teemed.
Here metal shelves and racks on caster wheels,
'neath severed tapered hands and bloodied heels,
There steel and leather couch, black chairs to match,
Surrounded by more art than eyes could catch:
A canvas tall as Dude was herein hung,
Huge scissors on a sea of red all slung,
A mannequin with apron and long gloves
But neither legs below nor head above;
A thousand photos tacked onto the walls,
All breasts and lips, stilettos crushing balls;
Workstations, easels, lamps built to be tough;
A giant television powered off

109

And flanked by speakers each as tall as men;
Footlockers, boxes, crates and crates again;
The towel in Maude's hands she rubbed and tugged;
And, 'neath it all, Lebowski's borrowed rug.
"My father told me he had made a gift
'f the rug you somehow schemed to deftly lift,"
Maude said, her tone and timbre still unmiffed,
"However I, in times that have long passed,
Myself had made the rug a gift, alas.
To my late mother was the rug endowed.
As such, my father's lease is not allowed.
So now," she said, then stopped. "Your face," (to Dude,
To whom she gave the towel where they stood).
Dude mopped his forehead with this spent bar rag,
Then listened as his host resumed her jag:
"Now as for this kidnapping business …"
She said, which startled Dude, who'd mopped his mess.
He made a noise to question 'xactly how
This Maude knew what was secret up till now.
While answering Maude moved to her TV
And from a crate pulled out a tape primly:
"Oh yes, I know about this 'kidnap' ploy;
I also know your role as drop-off boy.
I've heard it all; I'll tell you what I think:

There's something off, and high is this thing's stink."
The Dude could drown in all this woman's words;
Each one was spewed before the last was heard.
If she'd her way, he'd never have his say,
And so he blurted out at her delay:
"Right, Maude. But let me tell you 'bout this rug ..."
But hardly could he speak through her blitzkrieg:
"Mr. Lebowski, pray, do you like sex?"
She asked point blank, remote held to her chest.
"Excuse me?" Dude, astonished, dared to ask,
More checking what he'd heard than taking task.
Maude said, explaining, "Sex. The act of love.
Or coitus; do you like it?" as she moved.
"I w's talking 'bout my rug," The Duder gaped,
Intrigued, put off, and wond'ring what she'd taped.
"Not int'rested in sex?" she asked, surprised,
But even-keeled and locked on Duder's eyes.
She moved in close enough that he could smell
Her robe, paint, and shampoo (a hint of Prell).
"Do you mean coitus?" asked The Dude through gulps,
Becoming nervous 'midst the prints and pulps.
"I like it too," conceded Maude, blasé,
"Though there've been males that have been known to say
That feminists abhor the act of sex.

It c'n be a natural enterprise of zest.
Unfortunately, there are those whose pain -
A thing called satyriasis in men,
And nymphomania in women – is that they
Engage in it compulsed and not for play."
"Oh no," said Dude, unsure why she'd speak thus.
"Oh. Yes," he was corrected without fuss,
"Unfortunately, these souls cannot love
In th' sense of th' word th' angels are wont to give.
Our mutual acquaintance, Bunny, is
A poor and wretched soul controlled by this."
As Maude then turned away, Dude turned to th' drinks
And said, "You've given me a lot to think.
Look Maude, your mom's a nympho; that's too bad.
I understand why that would make you sad,
But I don't see what all this has to do ... Uh,
Maude, does this bar have any Kahlua?"
"Watch this," his hostess said to make him turn,
As pixels in her TV start'd to burn.
The Dude had found the fixings for his white
While cheap guitar jazz 'ccompanied the light.
With Maude before the set, Dude at the bar,
They watched a blond man driving in a car.
In oldish chryon font the screen displayed

The credits of the film that Maude had played:
"A Jackie Treehorn Movie," said the words,
"Logjammin'" punned the title, all perverse,
"Bunny LaJoya; Karl Hungus: Actors."
All this The Dude took in with bottle held
Halfway to glass, transfixed 's if by some spell.
"I know that guy," Dude said, vodka in fist,
"Shit yeah, I've seen him. He's a nihilist."
The man on film was Uli from the pool,
But with long hair and draped in belt of tools.
The scene'ry changed, the camera had new aim;
'Twas Bunny's place, and she skipped into frame.
To open up a door into her home
Where Uli entered, long hair on his dome.
"You recognize the actress here of course,"
Said Maude, whose gross contempt made her sound hoarse.
Back in the movie, Uli th' cable man
Conversed with Bunny th' undyed courtesan.
He said, "Mein dizpatcher sent me zis vay
To fix your cobble box mitout delays."
"Oh yeah, we don't know how to fix that thing,"
Said Bunny, hair cascading down in rings.
Quoth Uli, "That's why I'm sent; I'm a 'expert."
Then walked in coveralls all free of dirt

To amble over to the gal's TV
And slap it with his right hand expertly.
Just then a naked woman came inside
The room where Uli hadn't fixed, but tried.
"Oh, this is my friend Shari," Bunny said,
"She had to use my shower; hers is dead."
"The story's ludicrous," Maude grimly griped.
"Mein nom is Karl," looped as Uli lipped.
And on and on the dialogue was played,
Though little did it matter what was said.
Maude said, "Imagine where it goes from here,"
As Dude stirred up his Russian, milky clear.
"He fix the cable?" guessed Dude with a grin,
And with his tumbler finished his way in.
"Do not be fatuous, Jeffrey," Maude tsk-ticked
'fore with remote to TV, off it clicked.
She sat down in the chair that faced the bar
And said, "It matters naught that she's a 'star'
In pornographic films as her career,
Nor that she's 'banging' Jack Treehorn, I fear.
(That's 'banging', to use the parlance of the times).
However, I cannot abide her crimes.
Now, I am one of two trustees who runs
A program: The Lebowski Foundation.

My father is, of course, the second boss.
The program takes poor youngsters up from Watts…"
"Shit yeah, th' Achievers," Duder sloshed through sips,
Though careful that no substance 'scaped his lips.
"The Little L'bowski Urban Achievers, yes,
And proud we are of all of them," Maude d'gressed,
"I checked into th' account just yesterday,
And saw the million had been took away.
I asked my father where the money'd gone;
That's when he told me 'bout this abduction,
But it's preposterous. I'll tell you this:
No one has kidnapped father's little Miss.
This 'nympho', as you call her, clearly lied,
And took my dad for the proverbial ride."
So! Maude and Walter shared a common thought.
Still, none of this improvéd Duder's lot.
"Okay, but what about my…" Dude began.
"I'm getting to your rug," Maude stopped him then,
"My father and I do not get along.
He thinks I've made all my life choices wrong
And, needl'ss to say, I don't approve of his,
So this is how we live; it's what it is.
Still, though, I hardly wish to tell th' police
About th' embezzlement, my father's fleece,

And since you know how these kidnappers look
You can contact and gather from these crooks
The money you delivered days ago."
A worthy plan, but Maudey didn't know
About the Gran Torino which was robbed
Or Walter's dirty whites which had been lobbed.
Not wanting to reveal his hand just yet,
Dude said, "Well, sure, I guess I could do that."
Continuing as if her speech were writ,
Maude sped along: "If you take care of it
Successfully, I'll ante in your pot
Up to the tune of ten percent the lot."
Dude swallowed hard, "A hundred..?" "Thousand, yes,"
Maude interrupted, "Clams or bones, I guess.
Whatever you call dollars, they'll be yours
For executing this simplest of chores."
She straightened her red hair with nonchalance
With but a finger drawn through it but once.
"But what about my..." Dude asked, sitting down
Upon the couch which breathed its leather sound.
"Your rug, oh yes," Maude said without a thought,
"With your new fortune one could just be bought;
You'll shop around and grab what rug you see
With no value of sentiment for me.

And also, Jeffrey, I apologize
For th' crack upon your jaw dealt by my guys."
Dude touched his lip and prodded at his chin
To check his healthy jaw where swells had been.
"Don't worry 'bout it, Maude," he coolly 'mplored,
"It doesn't even hurt me anymore."
Alas, already Maude was scribbling lines
Upon a pad, all ones and twos and nines;
"I'm writing you the number of a doc
Who'll look upon your jaw and take his stock.
You will receive no bill. He's a good man,
And thorough," as she ripped and reached her hand.
As she stood up, as Dude spoke qualms discreet,
"He's a good man. And thorough," she'd repeat.
The way that she insisted made the Dude
Just take the note so's not to seem all rude.
"Okay. All right," he said, in brightened mood.

The deal was struck and Dude left in Maude's car;
Her driver drove Dude toward his home, not far.
While Dude relaxed, one foot up on back seat,
Dean Martin crooned a fiery big band beat.
The Dude, thus posed, still sipped the drink he'd fixed
While driver's voice was with the music mixed:

"So," he says, "My son cannot hold a job,
My daughter's married to a fucking slob,
I got a rash upon my ass so big
I couldn't sit to save a bowl of figs.
But you know me, I can't complain," he closed,
And thrust himself into his cackles' throes.
The Dude enjoyed the story, chuckled cazh,
And sipped his cocktail, leaving milk mustache.
"Yeah, fucking A. I got a rash," Dude quipped
As into jocularity he slipped.
"I gotta tell ya, Tone-Man, just before,
I got to feeling bummed and sad and sore,
Just really shitty. Lost a little cash,
Down in the dumps, my spirit had been bashed."
The driver, Tony, then surveyed his fare
In rear-view mirror; glanced, but didn't stare.
His chauffeur's gaze was aged and cann'ly wise;
He knifed a hand and offered this advice:
"Forget about it, y' know? Forget all that."
"Yeah, fucking A," the jub'lant Dude shot back,
"I can't be worried 'bout that shit too long.
Yeah, fuck it, man. Whatever. Life goes on."
By then the limo'd reached Dude's neighborhood.
He drummed his thighs because he felt so good.

What better remedy for whines and sobs
Than rich, angelic ladies offering jobs?
The sunroof, this cool driver; things were great.
With spring in step, no need to hesitate,
Dude left the car to make his way inside
Wherein, he guessed, he'd spend an EZ-Wide.
But just as Dude stepped out of his sedan,
The driver beckoned him with wave of hand.
Into the driver's window Duder leaned
To hear what information could be gleaned:
"Oh well, Mr. L, we're here. You're home sweet home.
Pray answer me one thing before we roam:
Who is your friend in yonder Volkswagen?"
He asked, then signaled back the way they'd come.
Dude didn't know, but looked where he was told
To see a small blue car parked down the road,
And if he squinted, if his eyes were peeled,
He made a fat man's frame sat at its wheel.
"It followed us this way," Dude's chauffeur said
As both men, far from subtle, craned their heads.
"Huh. When did he..." The Dude began to ask,
But quick, before his words could work their task,
Another chauffeur grabbed him from behind,
In half-nelson made sure his arms did bind,

And pushed him 'cross the street, not making sense:
"Into the limo, you! No arguments!"
How many chauffeurs stalked the Duder's block?
And toward whose other limo did they walk?
In Dude's free hand he held his cocktail glass,
Still full, aloft, and out in case it splashed.
Priorities! Dude had one problem solved:
"Hey, careful, man! A beverage's here involved!"
Across the street The Dude was frogmarched hence
To 'nother limo parked in prominence.
With 's other hand the chauffeur grabbed its door
And pulled it open s' hard it almost tore,
As if a dragon's maw by hero pried,
And sacrifici'lly Dude was tossed inside.
Dude landed sideways, hadn't spilled a drop,
Head-first he'd entered 'ere he'd land and flop.
No sooner had he landed than he heard
The Big Lebowski ord'ring, screaming words:
"Start talking and talk fast you lousy bum!"
The Dude looked round to see where he had come.
Just opposite the seat where Dude was laid,
Lebowski sat with legs in blanket plaid.
Beside him Brandt was stressed and tense as Hell,
Uncomfortable whenever his man yelled.

Brandt said, "Such frantic energy we've used
In trying to reach out to you, our Dude!"
Then once again Lebowski took command:
"Where is the money we laid in your hands?"
He raged with fists a'clenched and bulging glands.
The Dude was spinning; this was all too much.
How eas'ly he'd been tossed into this clutch!
He stammered for an answ'r, "I don't – Well, we…"
But quickly was he cut off, angrily:
"The kidnappers did not receive the cash!
You lowlife nitwit! You maroon! You ass!
I say again: the money is not theirs!
Her life was in your hands, you derriere!"
As if the point had not been got across,
Brandt helped, "Dude, this is our concern," for 's boss.
On the defensive, rashly turning wheels,
The Dude tossed a rejoinder on his heels:
"No no, man. Nothing's fucked here," was his case,
Which all too soon was thrown back in his face:
"Nothing is FUCKED?!" Lebowski's voice resounded,
"THE GOD DAMN PLANE HAS CRASHED INTO THE MOUNTAIN!"
Now thinking ever quicker, arming lies,
The Dude said, buying time, not locking eyes,

"Come on, man. Who are you gonna believe?
They've got the cash; we tossed them the valise."
Of all the words The Dude had tossed his way,
Lebowski picked one out that caused dismay.
He shouted, "WE?!" as if the word was new,
And at its very utterance minds blew.
A momentary silence hushed the crowd,
Contrasting prior maelstroms thick and loud.
Thus busted, Dude just puckered, ped'ling back:
"The royal We," he B.S.'d, changing tack,
"...the editorial – Look, I dropped it off
Exactly as per – Look, let's not get rough.
I've got some certain information, man,
And certain things have come to lightness, and
Has it never occurred to you two, man,
That giv'n the nature of all this new shit
Which, as I mentioned, now's out in the light,
Instead of running 'round and blaming me,
That, this whole fucked up thing, it just might be,
That is, it might not be so simple as…
You know?" he shrugged. He'd laid out all there was.
As eloquently as this had been wrought,
Lebowski asked, with consternation fraught:
"In God's name, what are you here blath'ring 'bout?"

Confused enough this was but half a shout.
'Twas all or nothing now, The Duder knew,
The time for hiding facets now was through.
The hand that Dude had held was being checked,
And so he laid the case that they'd inspect:
"I'll tell you what I'm blathering about;
Some shit that had been hidden's now come out.
I'd never stall a man of pow'r and wealth,
So here it is: your wife kidnapped herself."
A dumbstruck silence fell o'er both the men,
Encouraging The Dude to thus explain:
"Well, sure. Look at it, man. Young trophy wife,
In th' parlance of our times," (these words with grief),
"She owes your money all over this town,
Including to pornographers renowned…
And that's cool, man. That's cool – but all's I'll say
Is she needs money in a desperate way,
And so, you know, of course they're gonna gripe
They didn't get enough on this first trip
'Cause she needs more 'f the cash with which you'd part;
She has to feed the monkey in her heart.
I mean – has that never occurred to you?"
Dude asked, then added, "Sir?" to give his due.
At this display Lebowski had gone hushed.

He frowned and bit his lip and Brandt just blushed.
Lebowski lowly said, not lost of wit,
"No. No, Mr. Lebowski, I admit
That that had not occurred to me at all."
And Brandt, seized up, with no reserve of gall,
Said, "That had not occurred to us, Sir Dude,"
As if he read aloud the evening news.
His bombshell dropped, The Dude was satisfied;
They'd heard his case and logic took his side.
He felt expansive, sorry for these men,
And so the Dude absolved, best as he can:
"Okay, you weren't privy to th' new shit.
But, hey, you know, that station's where I sit;
That's why you pay The Dude, and speaking of which,
Could you use cash to make my coffers rich?
My one concern (my 'ccount'd know for sure)
Is that the taxman'll find out I'm not poor."
That last point seemed to not e'en register;
Lebowski pointed to 's seat's cohabiter:
"Brandt, give this man the envelope," he said
As if decree'ng a suffering horse be dead.
Brandt reached into his pocket and produced
A medium manila, overused,
Distended in the middle by its load.

Brandt, chin tucked in, leaned forward like a toad
And offered o'er this parcel to The Dude
Who said, "Oh well, if th' check's already drew..."
Dude took the envelope, retook his seat,
Unsealed it as Lebowski went to bleat:
"Since you have failed to achieve 'n the modest task,
The simplest of favors we could ask,"
(The Dude had then undone the letter's clasp.)
"Since my reserves of cash you've outright sapped,
Betrayed my trust, and with 't made my face slapped,"
(Inside, a roll of gauze, which he unwrapped.)
"I have no choice except to tell these bums
From you they should recover all their sums."
(Another roll of gauze wrapped in th' first one.)
"With Brandt as my sole witness, Jeffrey L.
I've this important oath I'll clearly tell:"
(With something firm inside, and rotten smell.)
"All further harm that's visited upon
My wife, my Bunny, my peculiar fawn,"
(This Dude unrolled, a trembling in his palms.)
"Will afterward be visited on you,
And tenfold that, by th' time revenge is due."
(Inside, a mess of blood and digit blue.)
"By God, Lebowski, now you have to know

That I will not abide another toe."
(In turning, emerald toenail polish showed.)

That very day, 'n a little coffee shop,
The Dude and Walter made a lunch pit-stop.
Now Walter'd heard the news about the toe,
And each man sat and stirred his cup of joe.
The counter where they sat, linoleum-topped,
Was as a field if pastries were its crop.
Throughout the diner families ate their meals
Amidst some kitschy 'merican details;
Some vintage posters, signs of diners past,
And genuine accessories of glass.
His coffee mixed, Walt knew all he'd need know;
He said, "You know what? That was not her toe."
The Dude, in shades, quite fairly could have been
Excited by what Walter'd said just then.
Instead, with fascination as his muse,
He asked his friend for details of this news:
"If this toe wasn't Bunny's, as you say,
Whose fucking toe then was it, I thee pray."
Now Walter smiled, chuckled, was amused,
Amazed at all the hackery they'd used,
As if a toe in gauze was some old trick

From days of yore when bands of thieves were thick.
He said, "How th' fuck should I know that toe's fate?
I do know nothing 'bout it indicates..."
But Dude had lost his patience, cut Walt off,
Reminded him, "The fucking green nail coif!"
Defensively, Walt raised his hands and brows,
And said, "Fine, Dude. It's never been proposed
That one could get some polish and apply
The stuff to someone else's toe they'd buy?"
He demonstrated this with tiny brush,
Invisible and yet meticulous,
And finger scissors cut a panto toe,
As cas'ally as cutting pasta dough.
"Walt, someone else's toe? But where the fuck..."
But Walter realized Dude's brain was stuck.
And needed some expansion with his aid:
"You want a toe? I'll get you one today.
I can get a toe, believe you me;
There's ways to get a toe most easily.
You'd rather not know how; one can't unsee."
"But Walter..." Dude said, hoping sense would catch,
Though Walter just ignored him, checked his watch,
Continued, "I can get a toe by three,
With polish on the nail, and then you'd see.

These fucking amateurs! They send a toe,
And we're supposed to shit ourselves below.
Oh, Jesus Fucking Christ. The point is this..."
But Dude just cut him off as at a bris:
"They're gonna kill her, Walter, then kill me,"
He muttered to his friend all sullenly.
So Walter hung his head to find the words;
He said, "That's just the stress through your voice heard.
So far we have what I would rightly call
A string of crimes with no victim at all."
"But what about the toe?" The Dude brought up.
"FORGET ABOUT THE FUCKING TOE!" abrupt
And loud came Walter's vulgar stern retort,
's he slammed the counter, rattling spoon and fork.
Each guest inside the diner turned his head,
Half at the noisy brute, half what he'd said.
A waitress, in her matronly grandeur,
Intending just to keep her workplace pure,
Marched over to where Walter sat with Dude,
And told Walt so direct 'twas nearly rude:
"Could you please keep your voices soft and gaunt?
This is, aft'r all, a family restaurant."
Perturbed by this, then Walter fired back
(Forgetting Dude as was, at times, his knack):

"Excuse me, dear. I've got some news for you;
This nation's constitution's nothing new,
And our own Supreme Court roundly rejects
Prior restraint! That's balance for your checks."
Annoyed by this, Dude stunted Walter's swing:
"Hey Walter, this in't a first amendment thing."
This lady, silver haircut glowing bright,
Took 'vantage as momentum helped her plight:
"If you two do not keep it down, I grieve,
I'll kindly have to ask you stand and leave."
Desiring anything but talk of toes,
With rage and pointing, Walt grew uncomposed:
"Hey, listen lady. I got friends who died
Face-down in muck just so both you and I
Could freely know the joy 'f a place like this;
A 'family restaurant', as you said, Miss."
The Dude had played this game and knew this song;
He'd rolled alongside Walter far too long.
'Twas obvious he'd not discuss the crimes
In which both he and Dude were intertwined.
The Dude got off his stool and fished out change,
Said, "Fuck it, man. I must, this place, estrange,"
And headed for the exit, walking quick,
As Walt decided whe'er to go or stick.

He called after his friend, "Hey Dude! Come on!
Don't run away from this until we've won!
This thing affects us all, man!" Walter pled
While customers and waiters shook their heads.
Walt looked around, defiant as a mule,
"I'm staying," he proclaimed then, "I'm no fool.
I'm finishing my coffee," he wrapped up,
And took a sip of java from his cup.
Intent to let all know that all was fine,
Said, "Finishing my coffee," one more time.
That's Walter, at the counter sitting proud,
With purpose, if not manners, sipping loud.

That night The Dude went home to just regroup,
Smoke herb and drink some Russians on his stoop.
Inside his bathroom, tiny lights of fire;
A candle for each angel in the choir.
In dimness Dude had drawn a bath and soaked,
Regarding both his feet as on he toked.
A roach in clips in unsubmergéd hand,
And washcloth on his brow to damp the strands.
From th' other room the phone began to ring;
The caller's voice playcd as the message screened:
"Mr. Lebowski, my name is Rolvag,

The duty officer who graced your pad.
The LAPD's found your stolen car,
It's been impounded in our public yard:
The Auto Circus of North Hollywood,
Down there on Vict'ry, in that neighborhood..."
The news continued coming from the cop
As Dude, with smoke in lungs, had coughs to stop.
He raised his brows, a smile lit his eyes,
"Far out! Far fucking out!" he said in sighs.
As cop droned on the sound was sudd'nly slashed,
As if with bat The Dude's machine was smashed.
So splashing, startled, Dude peered o'er tub's edge,
To see what'd caused the sound of phone breakage.
Confused, too high to think, Dude saw a man
As tall as Hell and set again to slam
A cricket bat into The Dude's device;
Two others in the front room stood as spies.
Assuming these were standard vandals here,
Dude spoke to them, as one would to a bear:
"Hey man, this is a private residence!"
His voice caused all to turn his way, incensed.
In leather clad, they sauntered down his hall,
A tall one, then a short, then worst of all,
Came Uli, Bunny's floating nouveau riche,

Who walked some sort of weasel on a leash.
These three men in the bathroom were a fright:
Their leather, cricket bat, and rod'nt alight,
Awash in all the flame of candles lit;
The varmint nattered, Dude looked down at it.
"Nice marmot," he surrendered, too worn out
To handle this absurdness in his house.
With slackened mouth then Uli grabbed the beast.
As if to say, "You like this?" he released
The fitful creature into Duder's bath,
Wherein it screeched and swam a jagged path.
Its claws and teeth a fury 'midst the suds,
Dude screamed and rose to leave it, lest 't draw blood.
But Uli wouldn't let The Dude arise;
With hand on Duder's chest and devil eyes
He yelled, "Vee vant zat money, L'bowski!" loud
And shoved him in the wat'ry, frothy cloud.
With two hands Duder splashed, though impotent,
Because, alas, the rat would not relent.
And while The Dude was struggling, through the room
The Germans taunted, each a voice that boomed:
"You think veer kidding? Und making mit the jokes?"
(The thrashing Dude was cursing as he choked.)
"Ve'll do things you'ff not dreamed of, Lebowski!"

(The marmot, panicked, lashed out manically.)
"Ja, vee believe in nossing, leetle man!"
Here Uli took the marmot in his hand
And dropped the soakéd thing onto the floor,
Where its drying dance made water droplets soar.
His joint long gone, Dude cursed an oath and sat,
While on his floor the ferret sneezed and spat.
Then Uli, brushing back his ceding mane,
Screamed, "Vee believe in nossing!" yet again.
Once more, to cite an oath, Dude yelled out, "Christ!"
Inspecting 'round his lap, if it'd been sliced.
"Tomorrow vee come back und vee cut off
Your chohnson," Uli sneered as th' others scoffed.
Still frenzied, in a state of disarray,
Dude hadn't heard what Uli'd had to say.
"I SAY VEE CUT YOUR CHOHNSON OFF!" with rage
Did Uli then repeat so Dude'd engage.
So loud was Uli's threat within those walls
It echoed 'mong the angels' heavenly halls.
With that the nihilists had made their point;
Each turned to saunter back outside the joint.
As th' trio left, their taunts did not abate:
"Ja, think about zat; your poor veiner's fate!"
"Oh, ja! Your viggly pennis, Lebowski!"

"Ja, no more prick for when you needs to pee!"
"Und maybe vee vill stomp und skvush it, too."
And on and on as they made their ways through.
Relieved they'd gone, but frightened nonetheless,
The Dude sank back into his soapy mess.
As they walked out, the tall one with the bat
Homerunned a lamp that shattered at his swat.

The morning next Dude cleaned the glass and mess
And phoned the cops who'd been his helpful guests.
No need for them to hear 'f the night before,
He'd only need his car 'nd the case it stored.
He got the address for the public lot
And cabbed it through the morning, bright and hot.
Once there The Dude shook hands with 'nother cop
With clipboard loaded, black hair flat on top.
This uniforméd man led Dude inside
A labyrinth of impounded cars so wide,
So vast Dude wondered where it all could end,
Where cars gave way and L.A. re-began.
At long last this odd duo came upon
Dude's ride, which he'd considered fin'lly gone.
"We found her just last night down in Van Nuys.
Sh' was lodged against an abutment," cop described

And gestured with his clipboard at the heap,
Now dented, scraped raw, gashes running deep.
"Oh man, lodged where?" The Dude asked as he ran
To peer into the window of th' sedan.
"You're lucky she's not chopped," the cop explained,
"This must've been a joyride t' entertain
Some punks who'd left it once they hit the wall.
Here, these were found nearby when we answered th' call."
The cop produced a handle from the door
And rearview mirror looking rudely tore.
"Looks like they did a number on your ride.
You'll have to get in on the other side."
Still pressing face to window, try'ng to peer,
Dude said, "My fucking briefcase! It's not here!"
He sidled round to th' passenger door to pull,
And slid into his Gran Torino's hull.
"Yeah, sorry," said the cop, "your case is gone.
Looks like they swiped your woeful carry-on.
The good news is your tape deck is intact,
Along with all the Creedence tapes you'd stacked."
Now closed inside, Dude shimmied toward the wheel,
But stopped and gagged as foulness made him reel.
His nose was punched by 'n odor borne of Hell.
"Oh Jesus!" Dude exploded, "What's that smell?"

A standard question, if asked to the cop,
Who calmly let the explanation drop:
"Uh, yeah. Prob'ly a vagrant slept in there
Or used it as a toilet, moved elsewhere..."
Such foul disgrace to fall upon a car!
If angels live, Dude wondered where they are.
Dude tried t' unroll his window; it was stuck.
He threw his hands up at his shitty luck.
And hollered from inside his closéd car,
"When will you find where these car-wreckers are?
Have you and your men any prom'sing leads?"
With this, with laughter, th' cop broadly agreed:
"Some leads? Oh yeah. We'll give it all we have!
Just let me phone the boys in the crime lab.
Some leads! Ha! Ha! We've got their phone calls traced!
And four detectives just got on the case!
We'll take them down by handcuff or by gun;
They're working us in shifts to solve this one!"
This cop was laughing as he reassured,
"Leads," was the funniest thing he'd ever heard.
The Dude was not amused; he grimly moped.
He donned his shades and sat with posture sloped.
As cop, still laughing, happ'ly walked away,
He made clear justice wouldn't be done that day.

Resigned to this, Dude glumly start'd his car
And drove to meet his friends at th' alley bar.

CHAPTER VII

"My only hope," The Dude said from his seat,
"Is that Lebowski makes my death complete
Before the Germans vis't anew my loft
To grab my dick and crudely cut it off."
Back at the alley, facing not the lanes,
The Dude sat with his team and spilled his pains.
Plopped at the bar, Caucasian before Jeff,
With Walt in th' middle, Donny to Walt's left,
The Duder drowned his sorrows with his pals,
He with his Russian, they each with their ales.
And passively, perhaps with hopes to choke,
The Dude munched on some beer nuts as he spoke.

But Walter would rebut The Dude's chagrin:
"That's patently ridiculous, my friend.
No man on Earth, a Kraut or otherwise,
Will get near 'nough your dick to ably slice.
Not if I have my say about the thing,"
He said through puffs of smoke that rose in rings.
"Well, thank you, Walter. Now I feel secure,"
Sarcastically Dude said, "You seem so sure
That you can stay these killers' mortal tug;
My wound should be just pee stains on my rug!
This fucking thing..." The Dude trailed off, depressed,
As Walter, sad, breathed air into his chest
While know'ngly shaking his head, said "Fucking Krauts.
Guess nothing ever changes. Nazi louts."
'Twas such a shame the state the world was in,
Walt raised his brows and pondered at his chin.
A look of puzzlement crossed Donny's face;
"These guys were Nazis, Dude?" his thoughts retraced.
At this new question, Walter perked an ear;
He knew straight out, the answer was so clear:
"They're threatening castration, you're aware!
Is this the time for splitting petty hairs?"
Browbeaten, Donny hemmed and hawed, withdrawn,
So Walter filled the pause with, "Am I wrong?"

"These guys were nihilists," Dude butted in,
"They oft said they believe in not a thing."
Such heresy was more than Walt could stand;
All spirit left his face, he dropped his hands,
And stared ahead as if a ghost he'd see;
"They're nihilists," he marveled, "Jeez. Fuck me.
Say what you will about th' tenets th' Nazis had,
Their Nati'nal Socialism which we dread,
At least it is an ethos," Walter said.
The Dude lightly agreed, Walt's point was good,
So Walter tried to keep flushing the mood:
"Let's not forget – Let's not forget, I say –
That keeping wildlife in a covert way,
Amphibious rodents for domestic things,
Held, uh, you know, L.A. bars what one brings
Within, for, uh – that isn't legal ei'er."
His counsel spake, he sipped a little beer.
Such nonsense was all this advice Dude heard!
He turned, his indignation rightly stirred,
And asked, "Are you a fucking ranger of the parks?
Some human dog who thinks not 'ere he barks?
Forget about the marmot, Walt, you ass!
You miss the point of all that's come to pass."
Walt 'xplained himself: "We're sympathizing here."

Irate, The Dude bespoke his carnal fear:
"Oh, fuck your sympathy! No need for that!
I need my fucking johnson t' stay intact."
With such new zeal did Dude defend his dick
That Donny's face lit up with f'rrows and ticks;
"Dude, let me send this question o'er your way:
What do you need your dick for, anyway?"
This question, as is natural, was ignored
As Walter, sat between them, re-implored:
"You have to buck up right this minute, Dude,
For by your sorrow all of us are screwed
In ways which our own talents never meant;
Bring not this funk into the tournament."
The Dude then popped with pressure he had steamed,
And "Fuck the tournament," he rashly screamed,
Then "Fuck you, Walter!" did he add to this,
To make it known that he was truly pissed.
What man had friendships he has not revoked
Nor hands that he hath stayed 'ere pals he choked?
His rug, a wife, his car, and soon his cock;
All threatened, all held in some impish lock.
The Dude was left to wonder only why
These fates befell a well-intentioned guy.
He'd no ambition t' steer an evil world;

Just bowling, smoking hash, and ogling girls.
A stunnéd silence fell over the three,
Till stricken Walter broke it morosely:
"So 'fuck the tournament' is what you say?
Friends who would cheer you, this is how you r'pay?
I know your woes, and that is just the point;
What other men would sit around this joint
To coax you out of this, your Earthly Hell?
Your message hits me clear as any bell.
If you've no want for cheer, you've earned your pain.
Come on now, Donny. Let's go get a lane."
So sadly Walter grabbed his beer and stood,
And Donny mirrored well as Donny could.
Behind The Dude they left off to his right
And, mingled in the throng, hid from his sight.
Abandoned thus, and left in dire a mood,
The angels mourned the taming of The Dude.
With not so much a signal as a sigh,
"One more Caucasian, Gary," Dude did buy.
"Right, Dude," the keeper of the bar obeyed,
And dried the glass in which it'd be conveyed.
Concerned with beer nuts, rifling as he hunched,
In distaste Dude heaved one that missed the bunch,
And then lamented th' oft-repeated line,

"With friends like these, huh Gary?" he opined.
The keeper said, "That's right, Dude," as reflex
And served The Dude without presenting checks.
The Dude, reflecting on his sorry state,
Looked deep within his drink to scry his fate.
The rock song on the jukebox faded out
And "Tumbling Tumbleweeds" resounded thr'out.
Without a sound, without Dude's eyes to meet,
An awful handsome Stranger took th' next seat.
This Stranger asked, a smile 'pon his worn face,
"You have a good sarsaparilla in this place?"
This fella, though old, betrayed a sublime grace.
"Sioux City Sarsaparilla?" Gary asked.
"Sure, that's a good'n," Stranger, joy unmasked,
Said broadly as he winked an eye and smiled
(He'd not had any drink in quite a while).
The Stranger took his time and looked around,
Enjoying all the sights and every sound.
His weathered face and hair untouched by dyes
Had nothing on the age that graced his eyes.
One look in these was all one'd need t' convince
That he'd seen ages past and all days since.
Content, these eyes found our man, squinted shrewd;
The Stranger opened, "How ya doin' there, Dude?"

The Dude, unfazed, stared down into his drink.
His brain so full, he hadn't time to think
About this out-of-place new friend he'd made.
"Ah, not so good, man," casually he said.
The Stranger, of a heart and mind that felt
Each man should be content with th' hand he's dealt,
Made stiff his bottom lip and curled his 'stache,
Which domineered his face like a scarf of ash.
"One a those days, huh?" The Stranger seemed to know,
"A wiser man than me had this to sow:
'Sometimes you eat the bar,' he said, but then,
'Well, sometimes th' bar eats you'," said Dude's new friend.
This koan seemed to Dude a mystic test.
"Is that some kinda Eastern thing?" he guessed.
"Far from it," quoth the Stranger from the West.
Within that moment Gary brought a drink;
He set the root beer down with but a clink.
With bottle stood before him, th' Stranger grinned,
And offered, "Much obliged," 's he touched his brim.
After a sip to taste the stuff, lips curled,
As if it was the last drink in the world.
The Stranger seemed to love all things on Earth,
For everything he touched inspired mirth.
He sucked his whiskers dry and, with a smile,

Said to his comp'ny, "Dude, I like your style."
And this with majesty was overrun,
As if The Dude was this guy's chosen one.
The Dude was fin'lly snapped out of his funk;
He turned his head and eyed th' adjacent hunk.
He then took in this cowboy he'd just met
(He hadn't seen what this guy looked like yet),
And saw this man was genuinely gruff,
Not some young Hollywood poseur in Western stuff.
From cowboy hat down to his rattler boots,
The Stranger made good on his prairie roots.
"I like your style, too," Dude said, mind like dawn,
"Got that whole cowboy motif going on."
From just as low and fearful as he'd been
In his whole life, The Dude felt his mood spin.
Sometimes to get your mind off life's tough breaks
The strangeness of a Stranger's all it takes.
This Stranger thanked The Dude and took a quaff,
And smiled, noticing Dude's funk was off.
Again he relished in the soda sweet,
As if, while drinking, th' day's work was complete.
His bottle then restored to its bartop place,
He turned his head; met Duder face-to-face,
And said, "Just one thing, Dude, that need be heard:

D' ya have to use so many cussing words?"
The Dude was sure that he'd just met this man,
And all their conversation he could scan
And not recall a 'cuss' at all throughout,
So he asked, "What the fuck 're you talking 'bout?"
Indulgently The Stranger chuckled then
And said, "Okay, have it your way, my friend."
He pushed himself away from th' bar and stood,
Then waved and grinned, "You take her easy, Dude."
"Oh yeah, thanks man," punch drunk The Dude replied,
And squinted as the man left out behind.
Not happy then, but neutral Duder seemed,
As if he'd touched a commonplace moonbeam.
The jukebox faded out its western song
And, just like that, The Stranger too was gone.
The Dude could sit and contemplate this tryst
For hours and all his blues would not be missed.
Alas, before he thought, a phone was slammed
In front of him by Gary's able hand.
"We've got a call for you, Dude," Gary said
As Dude breathed out some cobwebs from his head.
His mind aloft with nowhere yet to land,
The Dude took the receiver in his hand.
"...Hello?" he asked, unsure who'd even call

At this, the place where he and friends heaved ball.
Then, "Jeffrey, you have not gone to the doc,"
Said Maude on th' line, voice even as a clock.
The Dude was glad to hear her friendly tones
And not some villain out to grind his bones.
"Oh yeah, I haven't, uh..." he managed out,
The wellness of his jaw not 't all in doubt.
The subject dropped, Maude then went on to say,
"I need to see you here, and right away."
With nothing else to do, Dude said, "Okay."

At Maude's big downtown loft some minutes hence,
His Dudeness broke his own day-long absence.
Now more relaxed, and ambling with a slouch,
He entered t' spy a man sat near the couch.
This man, his legs a'crossed and bald of head,
Looked he not up from reading 'ere he said,
"So you're Lebowski?" in a voice so shrill
Dude wondered if it was put on or real.
The Dude suggested that he was and crossed
Toward a chair to sit there with his host.
The bald man briefly took in Dude's attire
Then shook his head and grinned his 'stache of wire.
"D' you want a drink?" the man asked, curtly flat.

"Oh yeah, White Russi'n," Dude ordered as he sat.
"The bar's o'er there," the man said to his lap,
Not gazing from the magazine he'd flapped.
And thus, just as The Dude had found a seat,
He rolled his eyes and clambered to his feet.
"So what d' you do, Lebowski?" asked the creep
As over to the bar The Duder leaped.
But Dude'd expected Maude and not this schmoe
And so was hesitant to let him know.
"Man, who the fuck are you?" Dude brashly asked
Not hateful (though that trait was changing fast).
The man let out a laugh that split Dude's ears,
As that of a hyena crushed in gears.
"Oh, just a friend of Maudey's," he explained,
And turned a page as Duder scowled his pains.
Up at the bar and digging ice from th' bowl,
"Oh yeah? A friend complete with cleft asshole?"
Dude quipped as he prepared himself a drink.
Again the room was filled with laughter's stink.
In fits this wimp was giggling like a babe;
Dude asked "What do you do?" to th' manic knave.
"Oh, nothing much," came out the man's reply,
As if not having hobbies makes one wry.
'Twas at that moment Maude, with all her charms,

Walked in on them with groceries in her arms.
"Hello there, Jeffrey," said she as she raced
To kiss her other guest twice on the face.
"Uh, yeah. How are ya," Dude sighed, drink all made,
"Hey listen, Maude. This thing needs to be said:
Respectfully, you know, as you'll allow,
I gotta tender m' resignation now.
New shit has come to light, I fear to say;
Your mother really was kidnapped that day."
As part of her arrival to her loft,
Maude placed a torso in a manner soft
Upon a table at the back of th' space;
A mannequin, dismembered, pretty-faced.
"She certainly was not," said Maude in stride,
Not turning (to her station she was tied).
"Hey listen," Dude protested roughly then,
While stirring 's drink and walking further in,
"Just fucking listen on occasion, Maude,
You may learn something. Wouldn't that be odd!
Now I got..." Dude continued, but was ceased
By Maude, who'd not yet finished in the least:
"And please don't call that girl my mother; thanks,"
Maude said, which turned the bald man's laughing cranks.
He giggled like a pigeon would on 'shrooms.

"She's definitely not locked in their tombs.
I'm certain she's the perpetrator here,"
Maude said, and ripped the tag from a brassiere.
The Dude, stood up before the front room set,
Had not been 'llowed to share his knowledge yet:
"If you'd afford a breath you're loathe to give,
The evidence I've got's definitive."
So Maude looked up now that she was recapped
From torso's breasts, now with bra deftly wrapped,
And said, "From who?" to get down to the source
Of all this evidence The Dude would force.
"The main guy, Uli," Dude explained to Maude,
Eyes switching 'tween her own and th' plastic bod.
Maude's eyebrows crinkled, missing what Dude'd mean:
"That's Uli Kunkle? He of th' porno scene?
Her 'co-star' in the beaver picture? Him?"
She asked, not out of malice, not on whim.
To hear her say the guy's full name was big;
It meant she knew, in personal ways, this pig.
Alas, ever the linguist, Dude would speak,
But hit on the wrong question, fumbling meek:
"Uh, beaver? Y' mean vagina? Am I high?
That is to say ... I mean ... You know this guy?"
Her clothing mannequins in bras was through;

Maude walked back to the bar and said en route,
"I may have introduced them f'r all I know.
Do you remember Uli?" she asked the schmoe,
Who made his affirmation with a hum
And nearly lifted chin from palm and thumb.
"He's a musician, if you'd call him one.
Was in a group that went by 'Autobahn'.
Just search you through my crate there of LP's
To find their album, r'leased in th' Seventies."
All this Maude told The Dude while pouring out
A bag of metal wares that clanged throughout.
Dude shuffled through her records as was told,
A few brand new but mostly all were old.
In time he came upon the one he sought
And lifted out the sleeve 'tween brethren caught.
Yes, sure enough, the cover did display
The same three nihilists from yesterday,
All standing on a highway, traffic-dead,
All starkly Euro-dressed from toe to head.
"Their music's the worst kind of techno-pop
Where songs play on for hours 'ere they stop,"
Said Maude, "So he's pretending he's the sage
Who took my father's wife as his hostage?
Look, Jeffrey, you don't really kidnap one

With whom you've been acquainted 'fore it's done.
The whole point of kidnapping's that the took
Will not identify th' offending crook.
If Uli kidnapped Bunny, when she's free
She'll tell the world the man's identity."
"Well, yeah. I know that, Maude," The Dude explained,
Which caused their guest to laugh in throes of pain.
'Twas such a fit of giggling that ensued,
It baffled and infuriated Dude:
"Hey what the fuck is with this guy?" Dude snapped,
"Who is he?" pointing with the album wrapped.
"Knox Harrington, the video artiste,"
Said condescending Maude, half spoke, half teased.
Unmitigated tittering went on;
Dude stood and listened to it far too long.
Her metal dumped and all her chores complete,
Maude turned to Dude, efficient with her feet,
And of mind, too, as next she pointed asked,
"So Uli has the money?" fuddlemasked.
'Twas natural that this was to her resolved,
For she'd not known of Walter's whites involved.
Then pressed for answers, Dude need think, and quick;
"Well, not exactly," said he for this trick,
"This case is complicated, have no doubts,

Infest'd with lots of ins and lots of outs
And lots of what-have-you's, it must be said.
A lot of strands to keep in Duder's head."
As Dude went on, Maude's phone began to ring,
Though, 'nvolved with Dude, she answered not the thing.
Knox Harrington looked up to gauge her mean,
Then reached himself to answer with a lean.
As Dude went on repeating with his strands,
Knox lowered the phone and muted 't with his hands.
"If Uli doesn't have the cash, who does?"
Maude asked the Dude, through 'partment's din, abuzz.
This mortal question, Dude's undoing hit,
Was interrupted by their plaintive twit:
"It's Sandro, calling 'bout the Biennal,"
To Sandro: "E speriano, pal!
Di rivederte blah blah blah blah blah…"
He prattled on through snickers and guffaws.
Maude turned to Dude, "I have to take this call.
Do you intend to see the doc at all?
You have his number, yes?" she'd yet insist
Like crossing one more chore off of her list.
The Dude, with drink and album in his hands,
Not fully comprehending where'd he stand,
Insisted then himself, "No, really Maude.

The bruise is gone. The wound is no more flawed.
I've no more need to see the doctor now
Than might I have before I took the blow."
For naught he spoke, as Maude was scribbling fast
A tidy note she ripped and Dudeward passed.
She said, "Please, Jeffrey, make this stop your next.
I'll not be tied to d'layed after-effects."
Dude took the note, repeating Maude's own phrase,
"After-effects?" he puzzled through malaise.
How curious it was that she would make
A stranger from her doctor treatment take!
Maude said, "You have to see him right away.
I've written his address to guide your way.
He has assured me he will let you in
With no appointment needed to begin.
He's a good man, and thorough," she intoned,
Then turned and, smiling, grabbed the other phone.
A flurry of Italian fluently
Spilled out of her and Knox with horrid glee.
She tittered, he laughed harder, so did she.
What strange and flighty birds these artists be!

So, what the fuck, The Dude drove to the place.
Why not have some free doctor check his face?

He found himself on vinyl table sat
While E. Costello through his headphones spat.
His Nepalese physician circled round
And lifted one phone, leaking tinny sound.
The Dude, till then relaxed, op'ned both his eyes
As doc, with otoscope, his ear surmised.
Relaxed again, The Dude slouched further still
And let the doctor probe him as docs will.
Then all at once the doc came to his front
And asked, "Slide down your shorts, please," rather blunt.
"Uh, no, she hit me here," Dude said with awe,
And dumbly pointed at his lower jaw.
"I understand," the doctor did retort
Then asked again, "Could you slide down your shorts?"
And just like that, for r'porting he'd been punched,
Upon The Dude a phys'cal exam was launched.
Dude understood it now: this man was good
And worked as thorough's any doctor could.

His physical exam completely done,
Dude drove around and had a little fun.
Just cruising streets and sipping on a beer
And finishing a joint, devoid of fear,
Dude hammered on the roof with open hand

As Creedence blasted: Duder's favorite band.
His head bopped with the music as it played,
His bloodshot eyes well hidden by his shades.
Mid-bop he glanced into his rearview glass,
Looked 'way, then looked again a second pass.
In th' mirror he made out a distant Bug,
The same blue car he'd seen 'fore L'bowski's thug
Had thrown him in a limo two days prior.
Dude spied the Bug and toked, his lungs afire.
The roach was spent; he pinched it in his right
And flicked it through the window, out of sight,
Except the driver's window still was closed
(Since th' car was stolen that window had froze).
The joint bounced off and landed in Dude's seat;
Against Dude's balls it burned with Hellish heat.
Dude panicked, gripped the wheel, and yelped with fear,
Unable to grab it, doused it with his beer.
The flame controlled, the car not quite so much,
With swerving wheels and grinding of the clutch,
The thing careened headlong and off the road
Into a dumpster from which trash'd explode.
Thus stopped, The Dude, with shades askew on face,
Looked dazedly around this alien place.
Specifically th' pursuer's Bug he sought

To see if it approached, but it did not.
The thing was gone, abruptly as it came,
And Dude made moves to leave his ride in shame.
He tugged the handle on the driver door.
It wouldn't budge and Dude's mem'ry restored.
He sidled right across the ride's front bench
And sought his roach by following its stench.
Where driver sat not long ago and smoked,
Between the cushions loose leaf paper poked.
Where had this come from, this sheet which was crammed
Into the seat of th' car so often slammed?
Dude tugged the paper, pulled it from its hole,
And, high as Hell, blinked as the thing unrolled.
The paper, slightly wet, was filled with ink.
With each new word he read Dude stopped to think.
"The Louisiana Purchase" was its name,
Emblazoned on the top, by quote marks framed,
And under that the name "Ms. Jamtoss" scrawled,
Which lead into the words "5th Period."
The paper, graded 'D' and standard-lined,
Was by a Larry Sellers crudely signed.
Red marking over misspelled words roamed free:
"Cite sources," "Use possessive," "Who is he?"
This final question by the grader wrote

Could just as well have been by Duder spoke.

The Dude, once home, called Walter to report
His finding of the hidden homework sort.
Once that was done, Dude rolled a joint to-go
And drove downtown to check out Marty's show.
Some four acts in there played a heavy scene;
Dude's landlord dressed in tights behind a screen
Blocked out his face with arms as if sun burned
Into the eyes of Adam daring to learn.
Some strings and horns from speakers blasted cries
As clumsy Marty w's cast from Paradise.
No longer hidden from the crowd by sheets
(Two hundred chairs, a dozen in the seats),
Round Marty was displayed for all to see:
A skintone suit and fig leaves covered he
But every bulge and sinew was in sight,
And every awkward movement borne of fright
Instead of grace was shown before his friends,
A dozen souls who prayed a thousand ends.
Now Marty, having rolled, was on his feet
And giant-stepping o'er to Wagner's beat
To step up on a chair and almost spill,
And gaze into a light as from a hill.

Among the dozen Dude watched solemnly.
Each passing moment caused his high to flee.
All new interpretations he would parse
Were in their turn unproven by this farce.
Still, all was calm here, so he 'njoyed the chance
To pay five bucks and watch his landlord dance.
Behind him then did Walt and Donny slide;
In th' furthest back of rows did th' trio hide.
Now Donny, on Dude's right, took in the show
While Walter, in a suit, leaned in, spoke low,
"He lives in Radford on North Hollywood,
Right near the In-N-Out Burg'r's neighborhood..."
"The In-N-Out's on Camrose," c'rrected Dude.
"It's near the In-N-Out," said Walter, shrewd.
"The burgers there are good, Walt," Donny said,
And "Shut the fuck up, Donny," Walt relayed,
Continuing, "The kid is in ninth grade.
And Dude, prepare ye to become dismayed...
His father is the man with given name
Of Arthur Digby Sellers. He of fame!"
Still quiet, down in hushéd tones, Dude asked,
"Well who the fuck is that?" as Walter basked.
The very question seemed to Walter odd;
He gave a what-did-you-just-ask-me? nod.

So Dude repeated softly, "Who the fuck
Is Arthur Digby Sellers? Some rich schmuck?"
Unnerved by his friend's ignorance, Walt scoffed:
"Who the f–? Has your TV been off
For decades? Have you never seen the show
Called 'Branded' which e'en pinko Commies know?"
The Dude knew of that show so he told Walt,
Who'd not yet s'fficiently flushed out Dude's fault.
"All but one man died that day?" he hissed.
"There at Bitter Creek?" the theme he'd list.
"Yeah, yeah. I know the fucking show. So what?"
The Dude returned to slow down Walter's strut.
The stage was set for Walt to drop his bomb,
So "Arthur Digby Sellers," with aplomb,
"Wrote he a hundred fifty six ep'sodes.
The bulk of th' series. Quite a creative load."
The Dude agreed the man had paid his dues,
And nodded as his friend conveyed the news.
"Not 'xactly a lightweight," Walt belabored once,
Then said, "Too bad his son's a fucking dunce.
Go figure. We'll go out there after this..."
Walt gestured to the stage but was remiss
To find a proper name to call the act,
"...what have you," though politely, he attacked.

"And also, we'll be by the In-N-Out,"
Said Donny, to which Walter blurted out
With, "SHUT THE FUCK UP DONNY," in a roar
Which drew some shushes from the theater's core.
Embarrassed, Walter glumly hid his face
Behind a paper playbill from this place
Before he went on to describe his plan:
"We'll drive o'er there in your beat-up sedan
Which Larry did himself see fit to break;
We'll brace the kid, so we may rightly take
The million clams within the case he stole
(That's if he hasn't spent the sum in whole).
He'll be a pushover and we'll be rich.
A million dollars for some missing bitch!
And yes, we'll find ourselves in closeness to..."
"The In-N-Out," did Donny interskew.
So Walt picked up, "Some burgers, Dude. Some beers.
A couple laughs; salvation's almost here.
Our fucking troubles are over, Dude," he smiled.
As Marty's dancing spiraled on, reviled.

A city which the angels call their home
Has yet its suburbs built on grass and loam.
This Larry Sellers and his father lived

In a secluded 'hood where darkness thrived.
At daytime angels played in sprinklers here
But now, at night, they fled and left their fear.
So darkened was the road where Dude was parked
That not a streetlight or a headlight sparked,
But only dimmèd lights that leaked from homes
And splashed on lawns protected by their gnomes.
The Gran Torino Dude pulled to a stop
Was chained to its own bumper 'ere it'd drop.
It rattled as it slowed and nearly died;
The engine didn't blow up, but it tried.
From this, the car drove on the brink of death,
The Dude and Walter looked out to their left.
Across the street, in front of Larry's yard,
A new Corvette was parked with dealer's cards.
What little light it caught shone off tenfold;
When they built that, it must have broke the mold.
All o'er Dude's face did cold despair then wash:
"Oh fuck!", he said, "He's present spent the cash!"
Behind them from the back seat Donny peeked
To spy the epic bauble in the street.
"Oh hardly, Dude," said Walter, "One new 'Vette?
He's still nine-sixty thousand dollars yet."
The three men left the car as Walter talked,

"Nine-seventy, if no options are installed.
A dollar, with Corvettes, will take you far.
Let's go Dude. Donny, you wait in the car."
The Dude and Walter skulked to Larry's door
Where Walter rapped his fist a count of four.
The door swung open, dashing their night shade;
'Twas answered by a Spanish live-in maid.
She smiled broadly, greeted them with, "Jace?"
Considering this duo out-of-place.
Here Walter smiled as a salesman might,
His brown twill suit repugnant in lamplight.
Behind him, scowling, Dude of stiffened mug
Wore shorts and cardigan thick as a rug.
"Pilar?" Walt countered, "Fine! I'm glad you're home.
I'm Walter Sobchak. We spoke on the phone.
My 'ssociate here is Jeff Lebowski, ma'am,"
Said Walt the wolf, politely as a lamb.
Pilar, still smiling, wondered what this meant,
So, "Jace?" she asked again to gauge intent.
Now Walter, still all smiles, doing well,
Worked up the pitch that he would have to sell:
We want to talk 'bout little Larry, please.
May we come in 'ere in the night we freeze?"
Another "Jace" and Pilar lead their ways

Into the house where Larry wasted days.
Just in the entrance, Dude and Walt looked 'bout
As Pilar up the stairs released a shout
Announcing, "LARRY, SWEET! DAT MANG IS HERE!"
Unbothered, not without matronly cheer.
Throughout the living room there hissed the sound
Of air being compressed round after round.
They looked around and Walter saw the source;
He nudged The Dude with surreptitious force.
Across the modest, well-kept living room,
Past brown and yellow woodsy modern gloom,
A glass and metal cylinder did loom.
Brown plastic-covered couches before this:
An iron lung that blinked with every hiss.
Brave Walter, hardly phased by this display,
Nudged at his friend and gushed sotto voce,
"That's him there, Dude," starstruck, he took his chance:
"AND A GOOD DAY TO YOU, SIR!" did he rant;
A noise that, plenty loud, roared o'er the din
But failed to stir the geezer laid within.
Pilar, likewise untroubled by these men,
Said, "Please sit down," and walked them through the den.
The Dude and Walter sat upon a couch
All plastic-draped, inviting them to slouch.

Still plainly stuck in awe 't the famous site,
Walt asked Pilar, "Is he – Does he still write?"
"Oh, no," she shook her head and seemed heartfelt,
"No more; he has the problems with his healt."
The Dude just sat around while these two clucked
As if the guy was not by coma fucked.
"I want to tell you, sir," then bellowed Walt,
"That 'mong the Pantheon your name'd exalt.
A thousand angels at a thousand desks
Could never match your canon at its best.
We're both enormous – Branded, person'lly,
Especially the early eps we'd see,
Has been a source of inspiration, sir..."
But footsteps on the stairs caused Walt to slur.
Behind them Larry, all fifteen and dense,
Stood on the steps and eyed the men all tense.
"See down here, sweetie," Pilar called her boy,
"These man are the police," she spake, uncoy.
"No, ma'am," corrected Walter, still midpitch,
As Larry circled round t' sit opposite,
"We didn't want t' imply that we're police.
We hoped tonight we'd let them have their peace."
Then Walter turned to Larry and he switched,
He fell his crest and baritoned his pitch,

All business with command voice to strike fear,
He said, "That all depends on Larry here.
Don't it, Larry?" Walt braced, as mean's he could,
Though relishing that this was where 't got good.
He reached beside the couch and grabbed his case;
He snapped it open, latches in a race.
Then with a flourish, willing time to lag,
Produced the homework in a Ziploc bag.
"Is this your homework, Larry?" he intoned
While setting 'side his case and grinding bones.
Young Larry for his part did not respond,
As if with English he was not quite fond.
Again, with arm outstretched and homework raised,
"Is this your homework, Larry?" Walter hazed.
The Dude, impatient, failing to see fruits
Borne of his buddy's method in disputes,
Himself injected, "Look man, did you not..."
But Walter cut him off, for th' trail was hot:
"Dude, please ... Is this your homework, Larry? Son?"
Then Dude to Walt requested, "Skip that one.
Just ask him 'bout the car," did Dude suggest
While Larry blankly stared through raiséd test.
Socratically, though, Walter played his game:
"Is this your homework, Larry?" 's his refrain,

"Is this yours, Larry?" calmly asked again.

Unsatisfied by Walt's unyielding hack,

The Dude made this a double-edged attack:

"If th' car out front is yours you tell us now,"

The Dude commanded, Dudelike anyhow.

"Is this your homework, Larry?" Walt went on.

"We know it's his homework, Walt, you simpleton!

Now where's the fucking money, little brat?"

With venom Duder braced until he spat.

Said Walter, "Larry, you're unplainly calm.

Have you heard of a place called Vietnam?"

The Dude thought this new tack was even worse

Than th' repetition Walt had tried out first.

"For Christ's sake, Walter," Dude broke rank again.

Said Walt: "You're entering a world of pain.

We know this is your homework. Furthermore,

We know that recently you stole a car..."

"The fucking money, too!" The Dude exhaled,

's he watched th' interrogation jump the rails.

"Yes. And the fucking money," Walt agreed,

"We know this is your homework," Walt decreed.

But through it all the kid had yet to budge;

Just stared back blankly, Zenlike in his pudge.

"You're killing your father, Larry!" Walter tried,

A move that would make lesser mortals cry.
But Larry didn't peep and didn't move
And Walt, all flustered, back the homework shoved.
He closed his case and muttered in disgust,
"Ah, this is pointless. Fuck it! What a bust!"
He stood and said, "Plan B," then turned to run,
"You'll want to watch out that front window, son."
As spry as Dude had seen him, Walter leapt
And bounded to the front door, up a step.
Before he vanished out the door, he turned
And set his gaze on Larry 'ere it burned.
"THIS IS WHAT HAPPENS," Walter screamed at last
To Larry, "WHEN YOU FUCK A STRANGER IN THE ASS."
His threat delivered, Walter left the house,
With Dude left sitting meek as any mouse.
Outside was Walter mumbling, storming on,
Removing jacket, exiting the lawn,
"The little bastard stonewalled me," he griped
As Duder's trunk he deftly open ripped.
Inside he tossed his jacket and his case,
And heaved a metal object from its place;
A tire iron gleaming in the night
In Walter's hands; this truly frightening sight

Was hardly missed by Larry at the glass
Nor by The Dude who'd jogged out on the grass.
Like Popeye rambling, manically it seemed,
Walt raised the iron o'er his head and beamed,
"YOU SEE WHAT HAPPENS, LARRY?" Walter yelled,
Now charging to the 'Vette with rage unveiled.
"YOU SEE WHAT HAPPENS?" Walter barked again,
A show whose goal was causing Larry pain.
With vigor Walter reared the iron back
And smashed the Corvette's window with a whack.
"THIS IS WHAT HAPPENS," Walter hugely rasped,
"a'WHEN YOU FUCK A STRANGER IN THE ASS!"
He waved the iron while screaming to conduct
What happens when a stranger's ass is fucked.
Stone-faced, dead-eyed young Larry watched the scene
As Walter maimed the 'Vette to spite its sheen.
Walt brought the iron down upon the car
While asking Larry, yell'ng to be heard far,
If Larry'd seen the events that come to pass
When Larry fucks a stranger in the ass.
No glass on it was spared as all was cracked,
As Walter madly yelled and aptly hacked.
"YOU SEE WHAT HAPPENS, LARRY?" he would scream
Before destroying outright its high beams.

All houses on the block were now alit

And distant dogs were going into fits.

"YOU SEE WHAT HAPPENS, LARRY?" Walter gasped

"a'WHEN YOU FUCK A STRANGER IN THE ASS?"

As Walter battled windshield, screams were heard;

A next door neighbor vaulted o'er his yard.

In underwear and huge this Mexican

Called out to Walt, "The fuck joo doing, mang??"

He grabbed the iron during Walt's backswing

And from the startled Walter pried the thing.

The Dude watched on as this guy plead his case

And Walter cowered, huffing, red of face:

"I fuckeen keel joo, mang! Joo fuckeen freak!

Mang, high chess baw diss fuckeen car lass week!"

This wild man with metal fiercely armed

Looked rabidly about, intending harm.

"I kill joo, mang – I fuckeen kill jor car!"

He said, and dashed away with raiséd bar.

He headed for The Dude's ride, parked across

As Walter dumbly watched him, at a loss.

"No. Hey man! That's not his!" The Duder called,

Back from the lawn whence he had watched it all.

Alas, the Mexican could hear him not,

For blood was pumping and his head was hot.

As he approached Dude's car all screaming, red,
The back door opened out and Donny fled.
"I kill jor fuckeen car!" the madman raved,
And not a window on the thing was saved.
Until exhausted did he carry on;
The headlights, windows, mirrors all were gone.
The Dude and Walter and Donny left the scene
And grabbed some burgers t' eat in Dude's machine.
Regretting that these friends had even come,
In silence did The Dude drive each one home.

So back at home, The Dude got on the phone
And talked to Walter as he worked alone
To nail a two-by-four into the floor
Nearby and parallel to his front door.
His home was filled with banging, hamm'ring sounds
As his side of the convo came in rounds:
"Yes, Walter. I accept your 'pology...
No, man, this should be handled just by me
From this point on ... No, that's not relevant...
Shit, yes. I made it home from th' incident.
You're calling me at home ... No, Walt. In fact
It didn't look like he w's 'bout to crack..."
His hamm'ring done, Dude stood and cleared his hair

And went to grab a wooden straight-back chair.
"...Well, that's just your perception, Walter man...
You know, you're right. This whole thing can be scanned
To r'veal a hidden message. Let 't be known:
It's 'Fuck you, Walt! Leave me the fuck alone!'...
I'll be at practice, yes," The Dude just sighed
As into place the wooden chair he'd slide.
He angled it between the board and knob
So no shove in the world would do the job
Of letting any johnson hackers in.
So satisfied, he marched to the tool bin
To stow his hammer in its rightful place,
But noises stopped him as he turned his face.
The door, which had been barred against a push,
Was easily pulled outward with a whoosh.
The clatt'ring chair found stillness on the ground
Till it was kicked, restoring all its sound.
The disappointed Dude watched as his home
Was thus invaded by two guys he'd known.
'Twas Jackie Treehorn's thugs: the blond and Wu,
Who deigned to tell The Duder what to do:
"Pin on your diapers, L'bowski," said the lug
Who Dude recalled had pissed all o'er his rug,
"For Jackie Treehorn wants to see you now."

To which blond added, "Yeah. And we both know
Precisely which Lebowski we have found,"
He said, ignoring th' board nailed to the ground.
Then Wu tacked on, "Yeah, Jackie Treehorn wants
The deadbeat L'bowski," piling on their taunts.
"That's right," blond sneered, "so get your ass in gear.
You're not dealing with morons over here."

In Malibu at midnight darkness fell,
Which angels at their parties could dispel.
The thugs took Dude back to a private beach
Where darkness was by bonfires hotly breached.
Through black of night one smiling angel flew;
The fiery air lit her as she fell through.
Her beaming face and naked breast glowed tan
As backward, downward to the Earth she swam.
Before she met the sand, though, she was caught
In center of a blanket which pulled taut
And had around its edges twenty men
Who each leaned back to toss her up again.
Each middle-agéd man had wild eyes
'Cause coke and ex and sex fueled all their highs.
So up and down into the air she bounced,
This gorgeous naked angel worth her ounce.

And all along the beach the party raged
All shirtless men with women half their age.
Some manic dancers flailed and flailed some more
While the Pacific lapped against the shore.
From speakers on high stands Mancini piped
For these invited guests of every stripe.
His jellies in the sand, Dude took this in;
Had will to join, but where would he begin?
Then from the crowd there walked a handsome man
Clad in a blazer, pockets held each hand,
And casually, in mellow voice forlorn:
"Good evening, Dude. My name's Jackie Treehorn."
The Dude and Jackie walked to Jackie's house,
A sixties modern joint with light all doused.
This mansion by the beach with ocean view
Proved what a porn producer's pay could do.
"You've quite a spread here, Jackie," said The Dude,
Whose confidence among the swank renewed.
He took a seat on Jackie's couch and smiled
As, "What's your drink, Dude?" Jackie asked all mild.
"White Russian, thanks," Dude answered, feeling great,
Impressed by where he'd wound up due to fate.
The mansion of a millionaire like this
Was something that The Dude would hate to miss.

The couch that he had chosen faced a pool
Which o'er the living room held stylish rule.
The walls were windows; all were glass instead,
So twilight twinkled all around Dude's head.
A bar of whitest marble stood at th' end
Where cocktails were now mixed by Dude's new friend.
"How fare ye in the porno business, Jack?"
The Dude inquired, adjusted, then leaned back.
"I wouldn't know," was Jackie's quick reply,
As if the question's asked by every guy,
"I'm in the entertainment industry,
With publishing, polit'cal adv'cacy..."
"Which one of those is 'Logjammin'?" Dude teased
As forw'rd to grab his drink his body eased.
"Regrettable, it's true," said Treehorn, stern,
"Standards have fallen. It's been sad to learn.
It's video that is to blame for that;
Now any amateur can rent a flat
And borrow someone's camera for a day
Then shoot the thing for all his friends to play.
Now that we must compete with dilettantes,
There's no way to invest as we would want:
A little more in story, production, heart.
There used to be a saying in this art:

One won't get by on tits and ass alone;
The mind's the biggest erogenous zone."
"On you, perhaps," The Duder blithely quipped
While slurping in his Russian as he sipped.
"Of course," Treehorn continued, "it's been said
That one takes in the good with all the bad.
There's new technology that lets us do
Exciting things that would bewilder you.
Erotic software, interactive tales;
Wave of the future, Dude. And wave of sales.
Completely electronic," Jackie gushed,
Excited by this big idea he'd pushed.
The seated Dude said, not as sold as he,
"Uh huh. Well I still jerk off manually."
"Of course you do," said Jackie, undisturbed
Yet unamused, his laughter smartly curbed.
"Well, Dude, I see you're anxious for the point.
Well here it is: Where's Bunny?" asked he, blunt.
The Dude, still drinking, said, "I thought you'd know
About where your employee'd choose to go."
"Well how would I know?" Jackie asked him straight,
"She only ran off so she could escape
Her debt which she has owed me all this time."
He never made a mention of the crime.

"She's not run off..." The Dude corrected then,
"On the contrary, Jackie, Bunny's been..."
But Jackie waved this off and paced the floor:
"I've heard this kidnapping bullshit before.
I know you're all mixed up in this thing, Dude.
It matters not to me that you've been shrewd,
And I don't care what you would stand to gain
From Bunny's husband and from all his pain.
All that's your business; I'm not in that line.
But all I'm saying is that I want mine."
His drink completed, Dude set down his glass.
He leaned his body back, slid forw'rd his ass,
And left his head into his hands to rest
With belly sticking out above his waist.
He said, "Well Jackie, I can feel for you.
A lot of concerned parties want theirs, too.
There are a lot of facets to this, though.
A lot of ins and outs, as you well know."
But Jackie's phone was ringing, so he sprang
And said, "Excuse me," from the bar where 't rang.
Sublimely comfy, Dude just watched him leave
But, with him gone, leaned forw'rd to drop an eave.
He strained to listen in on Jackie's chat
But heard, "Uh huh", "Okay", no more than that.

He did observe that Jackie scrawled a note,
And ripped it from the pad on which he wrote.
He hung up and excused himself again,
And exited completely from the den.
As Jackie left, The Dude leaned right on back,
And let his host believe that he'd stay slack.
But after Jackie'd walked into his hall
Dude hopped onto his feet, each on its ball.
Gazelle-like, cautiously The Dude took steps,
And peered hallward to scry the mansion's depths.
He made sure Jackie Treehorn'd truly gone
Before he jogged up to the bar and phone.
There sat the pad that Jackie had just used,
Among more stationery unabused.
The Dude picked up a pencil #2
And rubbed its dull side on the pad to view
Whatever Jackie's jotting could imprint
If, on the page beneath, it made a dent.
And slowly then, but surely, he revealed
New layer after layer was unpeeled.
The message Jackie'd taken from the call
Was slowly shown to not be text at all.
It looked more like he'd crudely drawn a man
And idly endowed him with a three-foot wang.

What treachery was this? What was this shit?
If this was all that Jackie had just writ
Then why rip out the note and walk away?
And who had made that phone call anyway?
The Dude considered all these things, deterred,
Then jolted as in hallway someone stirred.
He ripped his rubbing from the pad and scrammed;
He folded it and stowed it as he jammed.
Dude made it to the couch in frenzied pace,
Then sat and leaned as stillness held his face.
A statue then, as if he'd never moved,
He left no reason Jackie'd disapprove.
His host returned and joined The Dude inside;
"Where were we?" he asked, "I apologize."
The Dude leaned forward, saying, "If I'm game
And can retrieve the money in your name,
What's in it for The Dude?" he coolly asked
As Jackie bent to pick up Duder's glass.
"Of course there's that to talk about," said Jack,
"Another drink?" he offered, walking back.
"'s the Pope shit in the woods?" affirmed The Dude,
Familiarly enough to not seem rude.
"How 'bout a finder's fee of ten percent?"
Did Jackie from the bar e'enly present.

"All right then, Jackie. Done," Dude coalesced,
"I like the way you do your business.
Your money's being guarded by a kid
Named Larry Sellers, heir to all 'Branded'.
He lives on Radford in North Hollywood,
Near In-N-Out, where burg'rs and fries are good."
By now The Dude had got his second drink,
And with a couple sips he made ice clink;
"Real fucking brat, he is. But you got guys
Who'll get the money off him if they try.
He's only, after all, of fifteen years
And flunking social studies, lapped by peers.
So if you'll just see fit to write a check
For ten percent ... 'f a million," rubbing his neck,
The Dude pushed off the couch and tried to stand,
And finished off his thought with, "Fifty grand...
Then I'll go out and mingle," but he fell
Back to the couch, a'sudden drunk as Hell.
With dopey eyes he looked around the shack:
"You mix a Hell of a Caucasian, Jack."
With venom in his voice then Jackie spoke:
"Fifteen years old? Is that some kind of joke?"
The Dude could not shake off his vicious haze
And slurred his words through stifling malaise:

"No funny stuff here, Jackie ... Dude's your man..."
Then Jack was flanked by blond and Chinaman;
"The kid has got the cash ... Oh, hiya guys...
The kid just wanted a car for his joyrides...
But all The Dude e'er wanted was his rug...
Not greedy ... Not in this to fill my jug..."
Dude squinted up as Jackie's image swam;
"It really ... Tied the room together, man..."
Dude dropped his drink which splashed onto the floor.
Then he himself, unconscious, too tipped o'er.
His face squished on the coffee table's glass
And angels danced his dreams 's he faded fast.

CHAPTER VIII

La nerezza ha lavato sopra The Dude. Più scura dell'asino di un manzo scuro su una notte senza luna della prateria. Non ci era parte inferiore.

In a cavern, lit from th' mouth
With its entrance all faced open to the south
Shadows cast upon its walls all huge and lengthened.
Into this one shadow sauntered like a Dude
Who danced in, acting rude
A tool belt wrapped around his doughy waistline
His cable guy beige onesie looking fine.
Shadow arching up past height of man

As he rattled like a can

His tools all swinging as his hips did gyrate.

When he dipped into the cave then

All was turned into a lane den.

B'hind the counter uniformed Saddam

Spraying some shoes with fungus balm.

Behind Saddam a shelf of shoes stretched up into the sky

Th' Iraqi's workspace had so many shoes they touched the sky

Dude approached the counter like a zombie

Smiled just as big as ever in each eye.

Was staggered in his loopy stupor by the shoe shelf,

Beamed at Hussein then, thought the world might melt

And, being that the shoes were just that moment sprayed,

Was handed two size tens to match his belt.

And with that he hit the stairs.

Black and white, the staircase leading to the lanes,

Stretching its height into infinity,

So many stairs, so many stairs,

Good for moving on, Dude found, while dancing out his brains,

Shoes gold and silver, twisting as Dude pleased,

And he allowed himself a twist as well,

Hips swaying as his tools swung in the breeze.

Booty bumping, fingers snapped,

The dance Dude did was jovial to its essence,

He moved like no one noticed Duder's presence,

For in this world were all his joys uncapped.

B'hind the counter uniformed Saddam

Spraying some shoes with fungus balm.

At the bottom of the stairs

There danced a dozen girls, a dozen girls,

Arms akimbo as they spun their whirls,

Crowns of fabric bowling pins hid all their curls.

(As they danced, their tiaras hid a sight!)

Big checker floor, red blouses and white skirts that lit the night,

On every woman's face a smile to make this trip seem less a fright.

(At their core: a Valkyrie displayed her might!)

On he danced

His stairs alighting then.

In a world of pressing cares

All The Dude could do to help himself was dance the dance of men.

And it was Maude who played the Viking, it was Maude;
Her hair in pigtails washing o'er her chest,
With a golden bowling ball to co'er each breast,
She held a trident up like some Norse god.
A hornéd helmet on her head did rest.
So who had hewn this vest?

And back into the crowd of dancers strode this Maude –
The dancers rushing seamlessly in all their lines.
And as The Dude was busting seams out – busting quite a move,
While he was moving down the stairs he trod,
That's when he found his groove.
And in this groove he listened to his heart, its pines,
As he was dancing then.
And striding Maude the Viking, striding Maude,
Cast such a figure in her bone and gold
(Was all this from Dude's mind, or angel-told?)
Was this amour Dude could feel
That made his dream too real?
Dancers turned their turns so graceful, and teemed around their Maude.
Of dancers, was Dude best?
And how well did he move?

So it was; Maude was in the center of these girls,

Each one an angel in a pinny crown,

Each with her hands upon her closest neighbors' shoulders,

And from above they seemed a spinning rose,

Maude at the pulsing middle was their bud.

On the floor The Dude, in triumph, held aloft a ball

In his stout fingers

A king .. proud .. though put through wringers,

Stood there by Maude, walked behind her with ball.

Ball then lowered, raised his free hand ever higher,

From her shoulder to her hands with loins afire,

He picked up her arm in his arm, arm in hand.

Bent her arm at the crook, (she'd not resist), and pressed himself against her,

Gave her the ball then – in hand so lithe, tender.

Dude then guided back her arm and taught her softly

Then both The Dude and his Valk'rie spun the ball in circles loft'ly

And let go, as he had planned.

And while The Dude was teaching, all that time,

While he was softly teaching Maude to bowl,

And while they bonded then, and while he led her to some goal,

While Dude and Maude embraced,

All the dancers filed, scant'ly chaste,

Marched in lines with hands on hips down th' only lane,

Their red stilettos clicking on the panels,

And each, once in place and set, ready to leap,

Jumped up and split her legs, stood bestride the lane,

Each one jumping upon the jump before,

And formed a leggy tunnel all th' way down the lane,

Their legs the tunnel's frame.

And as the ball was loosed then, at the time,

And Dude's embrace was broke,

Dude now was floating, hov'ring, sailing himself 'bove the tunneled wood,

'Neath all the women, brushing their skirt seams, down toward the pins he smoothly soared,

And smiled, and thanked the Lord –

But! Then a great idea came into his head:

What if The Dude could rotate, facing up, and see between each dancer's legs?

And as his muse had spoke,

He watched, smiling the smile that he had found,

And knew it was so victimless, this crime,

This leering in his mind.

Lo! Dude had seen an eyeful and spun back around,
And looked he down the lane, down to the pins,
Then was reminded how a bowler wins.
His progress toward the pins was slow and true;
They were coming, Dude dropped op'n his mouth,
Tried to scream, couldn't, no sound would come out.
High as The Dude was, things were going south.
The pins were then nearby Dude's face about
And, all apart, they blew.

In the night ... In the night ...
Topless angel falls from high as Heaven's flight.

In the darkness Dude heard shears. Were those scissors then that split?
All at once the nihilists came, each dressed in red outfit,
Bearing scissors all, each pair as big as shit.
They ran to Dude, and Dude then turned to run.

Dude just knew the nihilists would want his dick,
Wielding their big scissors like maniacs,
Duder ran for his johnson from these hacks.

As he ran he couldn't seem to lose these guys,
Until they faded from him in the night,
And, running, slowly Dude regained his sight.

CHAPTER IX

As darkness then gave way to heated air,
The Dude kept running, hardly knowing where.
The cruelness of the scissors' sounds was gone,
Replaced by passing cars and honking horns,
And o'er again the lights that he could see
Turned out to be headlights surrounding he.
He ran on blearily, hands groped the way,
The middle of th' Pacific Coast Highway.
With the bloo-whup of tap upon its siren,
A squad car pulled behind him, gumballs firing.
The Dude was loaded in the cruiser's back,
Tossed in like luggage, baggy body slack.

With every turn the car took, Dude's head lolled;
He slurred the words to "Branded" as they rolled:

> *He was innocent...*
> *Not a charge was true...*
> *And they say he ran away...*
> *Branded!*

At their headquarters cops dragged in The Dude;
Into the chief's main office was he threw'd.
He bounced right off the desk, he'd hit it square,
And seated, more or less, he in a chair.
The Malibu police chief'd seen this fall;
As Dude was thrust he'd barely moved at all
Except to lift his coffee cup and save
Its contents from some spillage by this knave.
The other cop had Duder's wallet out;
He slapped it on the desk like deckward trout.
The chief picked up the wallet, had a look;
Whatever bits he found, these things he took.
He first removed a paper folded twice,
The quality of which was fine-to-nice.
Upon unfolding it he quickly pored
The dirty rubbing Dude had made before.
With unsurprised disgust he tossed this note,
And, filing quickly, took a new thing out:

191

This was The Dude's Ralph's discount card; the same
Which told The Dude's Ralph-Number™ and his name.
"Is this the only ID that you've got?"
He asked The Dude, his hate as thick as clot.
"I know my rights," The Dude took pains to say,
Leaned forward, on a desk-gripped hand did weigh,
And moaned as th' poison slowly 'llowed relief.
"You don't know shit, Lebowski," growled the chief.
The Dude, his head a'clearing, persevered:
"I want a fucking lawyer, man," he sneered,
"I want Bill Kunsler," said he, faux irate,
Not grasping when exactly was the date.
He pointed up at nothing to relate.
The chief, all settled back with mug in hands,
Laid down the groundwork for his reprimands:
"Now Mr. Treehorn told us you got wrecked,
And from his garden party they'd eject
Such drunken and abusive men as you."
The Dude, defensive, begged when he was through:
"That guy treats objects like they're women, man,"
He drooled, his face at rest on his left hand.
The chief bespoke a rage with just his eyes,
And talked as if to cruelly hypnotize:
"Our Mr. Treehorn is a man renowned;

He draws a lot of water in this town.
You don't draw shit, Lebowski, this I see.
We've got a quiet beach community.
It's nice here too. Some happiness? You buy it.
Now I intend to keep it nice and quiet.
I do not like you sucking 'round this town,
And bothering our citizens, you clown;
I do not like your jerkoff name, you waste;
I also do not like your jerkoff face;
I do not like jerkoff behavior, see?
I don't like you, jerkoff. You hearing me?"
By then The Dude had gained his senses back;
His brain by numbness no longer was wracked.
He sat up in the chair, surveyed the chief,
And blankly puzzled in his disbelief.
"Sorry," said The Dude defiantly,
"I wasn't listening," flat as could be.
Without a warning, quickly fired up,
The chief hauled back and heaved his coffee cup.
His aim was true, though clearly he saw red;
The thing clanked squarely on The Dude's forehead.
Astonished, injured, Dude raised both his hands
And clutched the place where coffee mug did land,
Then, "Ow! You fucking fascist!" did he scream;

He felt mid-forehead now a throbbing seam.
The chief got up and stalked around his desk,
And bent to place a hand on Duder's chest.
He shoved The Dude then hard to make him fall,
And backward did Dude topple, chair and all.
As chief pushed off he made his precinct proud:
"STAY OUT OF MALIBU, LEBOWSKI!" loud
And dangerously did he scream at Dude,
While kicking him and carrying on their feud;
"DEADBEAT! STAY OUT OF MALIBU I SAY!
KEEP YOUR UGLY GOLDBRICK'NG ASS AWAY!"
With each new kick into The Dude's weak side,
Dude wheezed as he felt rib and lung collide.
When chief was finished softening Dude's flab,
The front desk cop called Dude a yellow cab.

Inside the car The Dude surveyed his wound
And winced at every new detail he found.
The cab itself seemed wounded as it squeaked;
With every bump it crossed its carriage creaked.
The driver had an oldies station on
With "Peaceful Easy Feeling" as its song.
The Dude heard this and screwed up nose and face,
As if the tune was bitter to the taste.

"Jesus, man," he whined, his patience gone,
"D' you think you could put another station on?"
The driver, though, was downright militant;
Took umbrage at The Dude's tasteful intent:
"Hey fuck you, man! You fucking hate this song?
Get your own fucking cab and turn it on!"
The Dude began to gripe about his day,
But driver cut him off along the way:
"I'll pull over, kick your ass right out,"
He threatened, leaving Dude with zero doubt.
The Dude did not think his request was huge;
Just find some Creedence, something by the Nuge,
Hell, even Dylan would outplay this crap,
These Eagles and their sentimental sap.
"Look, man," he argued, "my day has been rough.
I'm in no mood to scuffle 'bout this stuff.
It's your car, usually you'd make the call;
I hate the fucking Eagles, man, is all."
The driver, looking back, shot daggers then,
And spun his wheel with hands end over end.
"That's it!" he yelled, "Get out! You're fucking through!
I'm not, in my cab, tolerating you!"
The cab screeched loudly over to the curb,
Its driver piling out in state disturbed.

With gusto driver opened up Dude's door,
And by his collar wrenched Dude to the floor.
His fare abandoned, driver flipped his light
And drove off quickly in the hazy night.
Dude, reeling on the highway, stood agog.
He craned his neck to peer out through the smog.
Dude couldn't see the taxi; it was gone.
He breathed out deeply then walked home alone.

As Dude traversed the highway on his feet,
A red Corvette flew past him, indiscreet,
All metal speed it darted down the span,
Its ragtop down, and plate that read "Lapin",
And unbeknown to Dude, who could but feel;
The speeding car had Bunny at the wheel!
She drove in the direction of her pad,
While screaming with the radio, singing bad.
"Viva Las Vegas" blasted in her ride
As o'er the pedals both her feet did glide.
Indeed, she pressed on homeward, all complete
(She had five toes on each her dainty feet).

At home after his hike The Dude surveyed
The damage that'd been done while he w's away.

His living room had been turned upside down,
Each item tossed that wasn't nailed to th' ground.
The carnage to The Dude's eyes all could seem
As if a hurricane had hit the scene.
Still clutching lumps about his lumpy head,
He lumbered on inside and felt half-dead.
He'd taken maybe three steps when he tripped;
Face-first and sprawling to the floor he slipped.
Still down and peering backwards through the shock,
He saw the culprit was the curséd block
That had been nailed so thoroughly before.
Dude flipped onto his back, now bod'ly sore.
Before he could make moves to find his feet,
A stirring from within th' apartment's heat!
What villain now or monster could be hid
To plague The Dude no matter what he did?
Around the corner, down the hall it came,
The final check to finish up his game.
He looked up backward, spying who it was;
His vision met with slippers wove of fuzz.
He panned his eyes back up to this thing's face
And noticed Maude Lebowski in his place.
"Jeffrey," said she, greeting her prone host,
Who answered, "Maude?" his sense of reason lost.

Then her command of "Love me," met his lobe.
The Dude, still out of sorts, said, "That's my robe."
As if on cue, she dropped it at his head;
Then Dude got up and took her to his bed.

"Jeffrey, tell me a little 'bout yourself,"
Asked Maude as one does ask when one's from wealth.
They lay in bed, the ceiling as their view;
What minutes hence was one was now these two.
Dude struck a match upon his wood headboard
And lit a roach which he had prior stored.
In right hand then he held his clips and toked,
While left arm under Maude's red head he poked.
"There isn't much to tell," he answered then,
"Initially I worked with just my pen.
Among a couple authors I was one
Of the Port Huron Statement which is known.
Th' original, of course," as smoke did waft,
"Not of the compromiséd second draft."
Maude, head all comfort'ble, resting on his arm,
Made active listening noises, parsing charm.
He smoked and picked back up, "And have you heard
Of the Seattle Seven? Of those words?"
She had, so he continued, "That was me.

Well, me and like six other guys, you see.
The music business briefly," he obliqued,
Which perked up Maude, her interest clearly piqued.
"Yeah, roadie for Metallica," he swore,
"Eleven-city Speed of Sound world tour."
Maude sank again back to her neutral state
And uttered, "Oh," at Dude's vanilla fate.
The Dude, still contemplating, took a drag;
"A bunch of assholes. Smoked a lot of shwag.
And then, you know, a little bit of this,
A little bit of that fills in the list.
Th' career has slowed down lately, it would seem,"
He understated, counting ceiling beams.
"What do you do for fun?" Maude asked him next,
Inspecting Duder's ceiling for its specks.
"The usual, you know. I like to bowl.
I drive around the car when it's not stole.
Th' occasional acid flashback I have seen,"
When, all at once, and like a laser beam,
A fiery spark broke free as he inhaled,
And burning down his throat the nuisance sailed.
He leaped from bed and coughed in heaving fits,
To clear the thing in tempests of his spits.
His bout subsided, then he met the bar

And plucked some ice cubes from his ice cube jar.
"You want a drink?" he offered Maude within,
"No thanks," she called and mid-bed moved to spin.
Still under sheets, she brought her knees to 'r chest;
She clasped each knee and held them to each breast.
In this position, gently then she rocked.
"What happened to your house?" she asked, unshocked.
"Oh, Jackie Treehorn's goons have made this mess.
To save the finder's fee, would be my guess,"
Dude answered. "Finder's fee?" asked Maude, confused,
Still rocking though her tone was unamused.
"Well yeah," he answered, pouring in a splash,
"He must have thought I had your father's cash.
He got me out the way to look for it;
Deployed his thugs of temperament and wit."
"It's not my father's money," c'rrected Maude,
"It's the Foundation's cash in that payload.
And why did Jackie Treehorn come to you
To seek the money which you ably threw?
If you don't have it, Jeffrey, then who does?"
She asked, collecting clues as would the fuzz.
"This Larry Sellers kid. Real fucking brat,"
He said, en route to where his lady sat.
"This case is complicated, have no doubt.

There are a lotta ins and lotta outs.
It's fortunate I'm able to adhere
To a pretty strict drug regimen to clear
And limber up my mind with every dose.
I'm fucking close t' your father's cash. Real close."
He leaned inside the doorway to the room
As Maude again corrected regarding whom:
"I say again it's not my father's dough.
It's the Foundation's. He has none to show."
The Dude enlightened Maude then, in his turn:
"What's that? He's fucking loaded. Cash to burn..."
"No, no," said rocking Maude, "It isn't his.
The money came from mother for the biz."
The Dude stood up and pointed with his drink,
"But he runs all the businesses ... I think."
So Maude then clarified things for The Dude:
"We let him run a business once. It's screwed.
He isn't very good at management
So all the cash he has is from me leant.
He helps administer the charities;
For this I compensate his modest fees.
He has no money of his own; poor dear.
I know he uses it to strike up fear.
His weakness simply's vanity, that's what.

201

He builds his own appearance. Hence the slut."
"Huh, jeez," Dude pondered, "So that means that he...
What is that, yoga?" asked he 'bout Maude's knees.
He took a sip, allowing Maude's relieve:
"It helps the chances that I will conceive."
The Dude exhaled but still had drink in mouth,
So, bursting o'er the room, did some gush out.
"It helps the chances?" Dude then yelped in fear,
Afraid of what he'd gotten into here.
"Well, yes. What did you think this was about?
Just fun and games?" she asked through haughty pout,
"I want a child," she explained to him,
As if he were exceptionally dim.
"Okay," he sputtered, "You should know one thing
About The Dude and what Dudeism brings..."
So Maude, amused, just told Dude to relax,
"I do not seek a partner for this task.
In fact I'd rather have the dad not be
A person I'd encounter socially,
Or fathom any interest, however mild,
In helping out to raise this precious child."
All this sank into Dude, who played it cool;
She'd found his bed and made use of his tool,
And now that their coitus was all through,

She'd keep the kid and ne'er again they'd screw.

"Okay, I get it," slow to realize,

"And so, that doctor..." Dude guessed, now made wise.

"Exactly," Maude Lebowski said apace,

"Now Jeffrey, dear, what happened to your face?

Did Jackie Treehorn do that too?" she asked.

But Dude's face was by puzzlement still masked.

Still miles away, he absently explained,

"Oh no, the chief 'f police in Malibu took pains

To make he sure they live up to their hype.

He's kind of a reactionary type...

And so, your father – Man, I get it now!"

Exclaimed The Dude, his eyes anew aglow.

He left the bedroom, went to use the phone,

As Maude sat up in bed, now left alone.

"What do you mean?" she asked out after him,

"My thinking had become uptight," he grinned.

He grabbed the phone and punched the buttons in

While Maude called, "What're you talking 'bout?" from within.

He listened to the line ring, tense, tight-lipped;

When it was time he barked in cadence clipped,

"Hey, Walter man, pick up the fucking phone.

I know you're there, as I could hear the tone.

Abandon me not to your dumb machine.
Emergency! Desist your awful screen!"
On th' other end then Walter did pick up
And, "Dude?" he guessed from having heard enough.
The Dude said, "Walter, get me in your van.
I need a ride, and pronto. You're my man.
But Walter solemnly said, half-alive,
"It's Erev Shabbas, Dude. I cannot drive."
When pressed he said, "It's Erev Shabbas now.
I'd drive you but my faith will not allow.
You shouldn't even 've called me, truth be known.
Unless it's urgent, I can't use the phone."
"But this is fucking urgent!" Duder whined,
Now flushed and growing angry, pressed for time.
"I understand that," Walter calmly spake,
"That's why I grabbed the phone. 'Twas my mistake."
The Dude was livid, screaming at the set,
"Goddammit Walt! You asshole! Shitty vet!
I need to get to Pasadena now!
Drive over here as quick as van'd allow!
You fucking prick! Your fucking Jewish theme!
Come here or I am off the bowling team!"

Outside just minutes later, on the stoop,

Dude pulled on him a shirt of sag and droop.
He walked out to the road to wait for Walt,
But something down the street there made him halt.
The same blue Bug that'd followed him around
Was parked there in the dark without a sound.
And even though the dark was made complete,
He made a fat and bald man in its seat.
Dude headed for the car to meet its man,
Secure that backup would come with Walt's van.
As Dude approached, the bald man leaned aside
In 'n effort to start up his little ride.
Alas, the engine flooded. He was stuck.
The Dude could see him curse his rotten luck.
Out of ideas, with newspaper in hand,
He hid behind the headlines which he scanned.
Unfooled, The Dude then made it to the spot;
"Get outta that fucking car, man!" Duder fought.
The Dude had to the driver's window bound;
He grabbed the paper, hurled it to the ground,
Then moved away as driver turned aside
To open up his door 'ere out he'd glide.
The Dude was startled by the sudden move,
And raised his fists to rain blows from above
(The Dude had no intention to use fists;

They just belied the fear of pacifists).
In turn the man, blue-suited, mustache thin,
Raised both his arms above his head to win.
This made the short man seem a little tall
Which, next to Dude, was not worth much at all.
"Come on, fuckhead," The Dude was taunting then,
Unwilling to let fear beat him again.
As several moments passed it became clear
That neither man had he a man to fear.
"Relax," the fat man said, "I mean no harm.
He low'red his mitts (this hardly made him warm).
"But who the fuck then are you?" Dude queried,
And why the fuck have you been following me?"
"I'm just a brother shamus," said the man,
Thus causing Dude to disarm both his hands.
All stunned by this, dumbfounded by that term,
The Dude had only questions for this worm.
"A brother shamus? Like an Irish Monk?"
Which screwed up baldy's nose as if it stunk.
"An Irish monk?" he asked, "The fuck is that?
The name's Da Fino, not starting with Pat.
I'm just a private snoop. Like you are, man!"
Dude wondered what this meant as his mind ran.
"A dick, man!" he continued, "Just like you!

And let me simply say, I speak this true:
I dig your work, man. You sure know the ropes.
All playing side on side, eluding dopes,
In bed with everybody; fab'lous stuff."
If he was lying, Dude had bought his bluff.
"I'm not a..." started Dude before he'd end,
"Ah, fuck it. Stay away from my lady friend."
Suspecting Dude had got the wrong idea,
Da Fino said, "Hey man, you needn't fear.
I'm not after your special lady, guy."
Attempting to sell solace with each eye.
"She's not my special lady," Duder snapped,
"The title lady friend would be more apt.
I'm helping her conceive," The Dude explained,
Just grossing out Da Fino all the same.
"Hey man, I'm not..." Da Fino raised his hands,
In hopes he could hear less of Duder's plans.
"Who hired you?" The Dude wanted to know,
"Lebowski? Jackie Treehorn? Bunny's beau?"
"The Knutsons," was Da Fino's answer then,
Which boggled Dude moreso than all those men.
"The Knutsons? Who the ffff-?" he started off.
Da Fino interrupted with a cough:
"The Knutsons. Wandering daughter job, you see.

Her real name isn't Bunny Lebowski
But Fawn Knutson. Her folks want her back."
He fumbled through his wallet to unpack
A paper photo, creased and worn with time,
Of a cheerleader, kneeling near goal line.
He showed the pic to Dude and side-by-side
They analyzed its subject as they scried.
Surely enough, 'twas Bunny in the shot,
A high school portrait marred by inky blots.
Here Bunny the cheerleader smiled wide,
Fresh faced, her Partridge Family hair undyed.
"Oh, Jesus Fucking Christ," The Dude bemoaned,
More pity than indignance in his tone.
"It's crazy, huh?" Da Fino asked his foe,
"They say she ran away a year ago.
The Knutsons said to show her this postcard,"
Producing one more photo, this one hard.
It just portrayed a silo and a barn
Amidst a snowscape on a cloudy morn.
"The family farm," his Brooklyn accent thick,
"They say that this will make their girl homesick."
With pity did The Dude survey the snaps;
Woe for the family stuck in snowcaps.
Their errant daughter set free in the West

Now made a living 'tween her ass and chest.
"Boy. How you gonna keep 'em on the farm
Once Karl Hungus's worked his penile charm?"
He handed back the photo to the snoop
And, pulling zero punches, spilled the poop:
"She's been kidnapped, Da Fino. 'R maybe not.
She's definitely not around if she's not caught."
"Fuck, man. That's terrible," Da Fino said
With hand besmoothing skin atop his head.
"I know, it sucks," Dude said, and turned to go
Into the street to see when Walt would show.
Da Fino said, "Hey, maybe we should link –
Pool our resources – Share what we each think –
Professi'nal courtesy – compeers, like that,"
He warbled, kind of desperate, kind of fat.
Around the corner Walter's van appeared
And toward the dick and Dude it slowly geared.
"Yeah right. Fuck off, Da Fino," called The Dude
Back o'er his shoulder, riled up and rude,
"Our short relationship is at its end,
And stay away from my fucking lady friend."
He piled into Walter's van and rode,
Directed to the Big Lebowski's abode.

209

Meanwhile, at a Denny's, in a booth,
Four nihilists were chattering, uncouth.
They screamed in German from their vinyl seat,
Too busy arguing (it seemed) to eat.
The same three men were there who'd stomp Dude's cock,
Joined by a scrawny blonde with scraggly locks.
She sat uncomfortably as they all griped;
Her footwear each was of a different type:
The left leg leather inched down to its last,
The right leg ended with a plaster cast,
Her foot was wrapped and looking not so good
(The tip of it was caked in dried-up blood).
A waitress came to make their order heard
And ended the cascade of German words.
"Ze lingenberry pancakes," Uli placed
As sourly the waitress then he faced.
Then, "lingenberry pancakes," said his friend.
"Sree picks in blanket," from the third of them.
The woman spoke to Uli in a hush,
In German then, and also in a rush.
Translating for his girl then Uli spoke,
"Ze lingenberry pancakes. Und a coke."

In Walter's van, Walt's eyes were on the road.

He listened to The Dude, who never slowed:
"We totally fucked up, man. This is true.
We fucked up everything he'd have us do.
The payoff was fucked up, connection missed;
We kept the case, the kidnappers got pissed,
And then the Big Lebowski yelled a lot;
His vengeance stopped short there, though. Did it not?"
"Sometimes it is cathartic..." Walt began,
But Dude was rolling faster than the van:
"If he knows I'm a fuck-up why would he
Entrust the safety of his wife to me?
Because he doesn't fucking want her back!
He's sick of her, of picking up her slack.
The man no longer digs his wife, you know?
It's vanity! The whole thing is a show!
But there's the money; why would he not care
About the mil that vanished in thin air?
I mean, he knew we didn't hand it off,
But never asked us to return the stuff."
"Dude, what's your point?" asked Walter, catching on,
As storefronts gave their way to gated lawns.
"His million bucks was never in it, man!
He can't get back what never was in-hand.
There was no money in the case you threw.

He hoped that they would kill his ingénue.
A ringer for a ringer you have tossed.
He kept the cash. It never has been lost!"
"Oh yeah?" asked Walt. "Shit yeah," The Dude shot back.
Between the shih-tzu's yapping from its pack.
"Well how does this add up to 'n emergency?"
Asked Walter as he drove on grumpily,
"I understand what happened now, and why.
He kept the money. He's a rotten guy.
But my point is, we're here, it's Shabbas Night,
In moving car with all lit up headlights.
The Sabbath, which I'm only s'pposed to break
If death's involved or life's itself at stake."
"Oh man, come off it, Walter," Dude complained,
"You're fucking not e'en Jewish, cheddarbrain."
At this Walt was astonished and appalled;
His mouth hung open, gasping at the gall:
"Dude, what the fuck 're you talking about?" he gaped,
As if his soul itself had just been raped.
"You're fucking Polish Catholic," Dude replied.
So Walter, palpitating, eyes all wide
Said, "What the fuck is going through your head?
I b'came a Jew when Cynth and I were wed.
Come on now, Dude!" he closed his little fit,

"You know this," he appended then to it.
"That's right," said Dude, "You're a convert. Of course.
Five fucking years ago you were divorced."
Walt scarcely could believe this petulance
And chided Dude for all his arrogance:
"Dude, what d' you think occurs when you divorce?
Is my library card no more enforced?
Should I turn in my driver's license now?
Have I stopped being Jewish then, somehow?"
"This driveway," Dude directed Walt to drive
And turning Walt, the Jewishest man alive
Told Dude, "I'm 's Jewish now as Tevye was."
More yaps came from the hyper ball of fuzz.
The Dude brought logic in as he could bring,
"It's just part of your whole sick Cynthia thing.
You fucking cave and take care of her dog.
You worship at her fucking synagogue.
You're living in the fucking past, my friend,"
He yelled, still doubtful this would fucking end.
"Three thousand years of tradition and tracts,
From Sammy Davis to Sandy Koufax,
YOU'RE GOD DAMN RIGHT I'M LIVING IN THE PAST!
I – Jesus, what th' Hell happened?" Walter said

Directing then his gaze to just ahead.
Outside the van, the Big Lebowski's yard
Had twin track marks as if it had been charred.
They led up to a red Corvette all smashed,
Parked halfway in the fountain where it crashed.
The Dude and Walter disembarked the van
While two steps back the manic shih-tzu ran.
As Walter got up closer to the 'Vette
He nodded at each dent that had been set.
Indignantly he marched to the front door
While Dude, himself all bothered, went before.
They crossed the threshold, clambered to the hall,
Where Brandt was gathering clothes up in a ball.
The clothes were strewn haphazard 'bout the place
While yonder Bunny doffed her things of lace
And naked dove into Lebowski's pool
As Brandt cleaned up her mess and played the fool.
He stooped and straightened o'er and o'er again
While welcoming The Dude and his large friend.
"He cannot see you now, Dude," he intoned,
"He'd much prefer to just be left alone."
He was mid-crisis, speaking at a clip;
The words had scarce been thought that passed his lips.
"Oh, where th' fuck was she, man?" then taunted Dude.

Brandt's jig was up, this line of questions clued.
"Sh' was in Palm Springs, to visit friends of hers;
She just picked up and left without a word."
The Dude, still marching briskly to the West,
Said, "Yeah, but she told Uli, though, I guess."
For how else would the nihilists have known
To ask for ransom when she wasn't home?
As Walter and his dog walked on in tow,
Walt said, "That bitch! She didn't even know!"
"Now, Dude. Come on. Who is this yelling man?"
Brandt asked, near tears, but working through the pain.
This stopped Walt in his tracks; he faced the man;
"I'll tell you. I'M A FUCKING VETERAN."
With that The Dude and Walter trudged inside,
Ignoring Brandt, as at their heels he cried:
"Please, Dude. You shouldn't go into that room.
He's very angry." This he yelled with gloom.
In the Great Room the double doors burst in.
Lebowski's chair was humming in its spin.
He turned to face the noise and saw these men
And bitterly he spoke 'ere they'd begin:
"Oh well. She's back, no thanks to you," he crabbed.
But "Where's the money, Lebowski?" Duder jabbed.
He used the very scansion blond had used

When first by toilet was his head abused.
In turn then Walter deftly flipped his lid:
"A million bucks from needy little kids!
Man, you are scum!" he pointed through the dark
As his excited shih-tzu leapt and barked.
"Well who the Hell is he?" Lebowski screeched,
Regarding Walt, who'd dressed to storm a beach.
"I'll tell you who I am," Walt melted down,
"I am the mayor, and Painworld is the town!
You'd better treasure each breath as your last.
I'm here to kick your fake goldbricking ass!"
As Walter seethed with rage and blustered loud,
Dude showed his hand and proved himself, all proud:
"We know there was no money in the case
And that you've kept the million at this place!"
Lebowski, thus called out, could only smile,
And parry it with hubris, coldly vile:
"You have your story, sir, and I have mine.
I say I trusted you and, bottom line,
You stole it. Took it to your bum enclave,"
He pointed, grinning at the pair of knaves.
"As if we'd ever dream of doing that!
Your bullshit fucking money!" Walter spat.
Annoyed, The Dude switched into tirade mode:

"You thought your wife was some kidnapper's load,
And so you had a pretext, nice and clear,
To make some fucking money disappear.
But for your plot you'd need to use some sap
To pin it on, to fall into your trap.
You'd just met me, you human paraquat!
You got an eyeful of The Dude and thought
'Well, hey, a deadbeat loser who, no doubt,
The square community won't care about!'"
With hands on hips he gave his case a rest,
Secure the Big Lebowski'd met his best.
"Well aren't ya?" the wheelchaired villain asked
To cut The Dude there where he stood and basked.
This blunt response The Dude did not foresee;
"Well, yeah," he couldn't help but to agree.
The line of accusations seeming dead,
"Get out, the both of you!" Lebowski said.
But Walter, never minding facts were straight,
Made up his mind to reinsinuate:
"Look at that fucking phony in his chair,
Pretending still to be a millionaire."
"I said get out," Lebowski growled at them,
Withdrawing in to leave them in their shame.
But Walter was not easily dispelled.

217

He went on, "Let me tell you something else;
I've seen a lot of spinals in my time,
And this guy is a faker. That's the crime.
A fucking phony goldbricker," Walt hissed,
Advancing on the wheelchair, slow and pissed.
"You stay away fr'm me, mister," Big L. begged,
Stuck helpless since he was not able-legged.
But Walter was upon him, and he grabbed
Lebowski under armpits old and flabbed.
Walt hoisted him aloft and swung him 'round
To hold him not o'er wheelchair but o'er ground.
Such a cacophony then filled the room,
As if the place was discord's very womb.
With Walter screaming, "Walk, you phony! Walk!"
His prey too busy squealing then to talk.
The Dude in panic also made his sound:
"He's fucking crippled, Walter, put him down!"
And all the time the little shih-tzu leapt
And barked about the room of he who wept.
Lebowski's rubbery legs begraced the floor
Like Raggedy Ann's would sweep a doll hair store.
"I'll fucking put him down, Dude," Walter yelled,
"Inf raus! Achtung, baby!" 'ere he compelled
The old man to the floor by letting go.

He could not stand, and fell like so much dough.
The sound resounded through the stuffy air
As if an angel'd dropped his harp in there.
Then all went silent just as Walter grasped
That he'd just let an invalid collapse.
The little dog ran to the man of years
And licked away a couple of his tears.
Dejected, Big Lebowski lay agog,
But still had strength to cast aside the dog.
His accusations having borne attacks,
Dude bit his lip, deciding to hold back.
For how could he accuse a man so prone,
Surrounded by fake wealth and all alone.
He looked at Walter, brushing back his hair,
"Just help me get him back into his chair."
Walt did, and then they left Lebowski's lair.

CHAPTER X

The pair returned back to the bowling lanes.
Though late, they thought they'd play a couple games.
'Twas Donny's roll; he bowled with perfect time.
His ball seemed true 's it lumbered down the pine.
The pins were scattered; Donny'd hit them well,
But one pin stood where all the others fell.
As witness Donny watched this with a glare;
It had been days since he had rolled a spare.
Dejected, Donny turned back to the bench
And grabbed his beer to drown away the stench.
Meanwhile Walter sat there with The Dude
Discussing all the ways Iraq was screwed:

"Well, sure. I guess you'll see some fights in tanks;
Some mechanized equipment in their ranks.
But fighting in the jungle would be worse
Than these spitball encounters in deserts."
"Uh huh," The Dude placated, keeping mum,
Applying clear nail polish to his thumb.
So Walt continued, "'Nam was really war.
A foot soldier was king o'er there, full-bore.
This thing should be a fucking cakewalk, though.
I mean, in 'Nam, we only had to go
Into the bush with but an M16
And not an Abrams tank to help my team.
Just me and fucking Charlie, man to man,
Eyeball to eyeball, fighting hand to hand.
That's fucking combat, as I've understood.
The man in the fucking black pyjamas, Dude..."
"Who's in pyjamas, Walter?" Donny asked.
So, "Shut the fuck up, Donny," Walter lashed.
Continuing, the storytelling vet
Pulled down his shirt and ashed his cigarette:
"Not all these goddamn fig-eaters in th' sand,
A towel on each head, and in each hand
A manual so they can find reverse
On tanks which were the Soviets' at first.

This adversary isn't worth our time..."
But 'fore he could continue down that line,
A shout of "Hey!" from up upon the lanes
Turned all their heads to see who did the sayin'.
Upon the lane stood Jesus, looking down,
Restrained by Liam, bellowing with a frown:
"What is this 'day of rest' shit, mang?" he went,
As Walter feigned a look so innocent,
"What is this bullshit you got going 'round?
But I don't care. You tell th' whole fucking town
That it don't matter t' Jesus. Ha! You see?
Your Jewish bullshit isn't fooling me!
You might fool all the fucks in th' league office,
But you're not fucking fooling the Jesus!
It's bush league psych-out stuff, man. Laughable!
Ha ha! Your fuck-up days aren't lastable.
I'd 've fucked you in the ass on Saturday,
On Wednesday I'll fuck your ass anyway!"
Then with his hips he made a coital move
And hooted as his partner led with shoves.
And as they walked away into the crowd:
"You got a date on Wednesday, baby!" loud.
Then Walter and The Dude watched Jesus go.
"He's cracking," Walter said, his head hung low.

As Donny, Walter, and The Dude walked out,
Walter still was rattling on about
Some random thing: "...the whole concept of Aish.
That's why mid-fourteenth century a fresh
New Rambam..." Walter faded out,
A'stunned by what was happening in the lot.
The three men stood with satchels in their hands
As orange flames licked at The Dude's sedan.
The same three nihilists, all leather clad
Stood in the empty lot, up to all bad.
One held a boombox playing techno schlock,
He and his partners standing still as rocks.
The Dude's car was, alas, involved in fire,
Down from its roof to every flaming tire.
The motorcycles of the Germans stood,
All lined up in a row by Duder's hood.
"Oh well. They finally did it," Dude morosed,
"They killed my fucking car. The thing is toast."
"Vee vant zat money, L'bowski," Uli called.
His buddies Franz and Kiefer all enthralled.
"Ja, othervise vee killsechurl," said Franz.
"That's right," said Kiefer, "those were our demands.
It seems you have forgot our little deal."

223

As tires melted over glowing wheels.
The Dude, though bummed, was also seeing red:
"You haven't got the girl! You never did!"
Confused, the Germans huddled and conferred
While Donny leaned to Walt to have a word:
"Are these the Nazis, Walter?" Donny asked,
His lostness and his fear all but unmasked.
"These men are nih'lists, Donny. Never fear,"
Said Walter in a voice defining care.
The Germans stopped their talking and regrouped,
And Uli said, "Vee still vill fucks you up
Unless you give zat money zat vee vant."
Then Kiefer added his Teutonic taunt:
"Ja, vee fuck you up. Vee sreaten you."
But Walt called, "Fuck you. Fuck the three of you.
If you have got no hostage, there's no pay.
There can't be ransom any other way."
Walt stood there tall, defying these three creeps,
As Kiefer whined, like gadfly-riddled sheeps,
"His girlfriend gave her toe up for her share.
She thought we'd get the million. Iss not fair!"
So Walter, now the leader of our three,
Screamed, "Fair?! You gotta be fucking kidding me!
Which group of us is nihilists around here?

Or are you just crybabies full of fear?"
Then Duder interjected, "Cool it, Walt.
Hey, listen, pal. That's not our fucking fault.
Lebowski packed his case with zero cash,
So take it up with his disabled ass."
Now that the conversation was on track,
Walt added, "And I'd like my undies back."
At this bad news again the Germans scoffed
And huddled up again to talk it off.
"Are these guys gonna hurt us?" Donny peeped,
But Walter raised a hand 'ere Donny'd leap.
"They cannot hurt us, Donny, with their words.
They'll not attack, this gaggle of cowards."
Again, their plotting finished, they formed rank,
And made another threat to make some bank:
"Okay," said Uli, "Let this thing be srough.
Just gif us all the cash you haf on you.
Vee callsit even then," the German shrugged.
A tic alit his face, he was so bugged.
This seemed to Dude and Donny fair enough,
But Walter said, "Fuck you," to call his bluff.
"Come on now, Walter, we're ending this thing cheap,"
Dude said, exam'ning what'd his pockets keep.
"What's mine is mine," did Walter still defy

Without taking his eyes off of the guy.
"Hey Walter, come on," Dude did yet implore,
Then, to the Germans, "Looks like a I got four,
Or maybe five bucks if you count the change."
"I got eighteen," squeaked Donny, out of range.
But Walter grimly stood and didn't move.
"What's mine is mine," with mettle he would prove.
A ring of steel sheared through the dark night air
As Uli pulled the saber he did wear
And brandished it at the opposing group.
"Vee takes your money, man! Vee fucks you up!"
With placid stillness like a frozen pond,
Walt goaded, "Come and get it," to the blond.
"Vee fucks you up, man!" Uli's yelling roared
As still he swiped and gestured with his sword.
"Come on and get it, nihilist," was Walt's stand
As he invited danger with waved hand.
Walt's bravery was pissing Uli off;
"I fuck you!" and "I fuck you!" did he cough.
But still he shouted orders from afar,
A frenzy between Walt and burning car.
So Walter wanted just to make it real;
"Just show me what you got. You know the deal.
Your fucking nihilism's not 'n my head;

You dipshit with a nine-toed frau in bed."
That tore it. Uli charged with sword up high,
But Walt was more than ready for the guy.
He windmilled 'round his satchel 'ere he'd heft
And sent his ball to smash in Kieffer's chest.
With such artillery was Kieffer bashed,
And heaving to the ground his body crashed.
One comrade lost, but Uli didn't halt;
Still calling out, "I fuck you!" upon Walt.
But battle-eager Walter was prepared,
And in two mitts the German's head ensnared.
With streak of light and such unholy sound
The nihilist's saber clattered to the ground.
The stronger Walter brought his foe's head near;
Tenaciously he bit down on its ear
And would not let it go for all his worth
As, grunting, did he worry it back and forth.
While Uli screamed and was all cannibalized,
The Dude squared off against this Franz outsize.
A seven-footer, German accent thick,
He filled Dude's bubble with karate kicks.
The poor Dude wanted just to pay this man
Who was determined just to make a stand.
When money didn't work, he tried this call:

227

"Come on, fuckhead. I'll hit you with my ball."
These two at loggerheads did swing and sit,
But neither man would dare to score a hit.
Still Walter, like a pit bull, growled and tugged
Until the ear from its own head unplugged.
His goatee stiff with gore, Walt leaned his head
And geysered up the ear in plume of red.
He spat it twenty feet into the sky;
Some angel could have seen the ear soar by.
Poor Uli stood distracted by the pain
Of having lost a holder for his brain.
With deadness in his eyes he stood there mute,
For Walter'd surely won; none could refute.
The bigger man drew back a fist and said,
"You anti-Semite," punching Uli's head.
'Twas such a blow that Uli's face did clot
And fell he bleeding down onto the lot.
The Dude had his man staved off pretty well,
Till Franz lost all his patience, gave a yell,
And charged The Dude, all poised to judo chop
When from nowhere a boombox hit him: "Whop!"
'Twas Walter wielding th' very radio
The nihilists had brought to this road show.
Again then Walter hit him in the back.

Franz fell, and thus was finished their attack.
So Walter dropped the boombox with a thud,
Stood hands-on-knees, his mouth still dripping blood,
And looked around the pavement, breathing hard,
To spot their Donny felled at twenty yards.
"Heads up now, Dude! A man of ours is down."
Still panting, as was Dude, they covered ground
And made it to the spot where Donny lay,
Half rolling round and hurt in a bad way.
"My God. They shot him," Dude with fear surmised,
His gaze transfixed by th' pain in Donny's eyes.
"No shots were fired as we fought them back,"
Said Walter, "This looks like a heart attack."
Now Walter knelt beside his meeker friend,
Committed to prevent his ally's end:
"Dude call the medics," barely he could shout,
"I'd go myself, but I might just pass out.
I'm pumping blood," he finished as Dude ran
Into th' alley to call the fixer man.
Walt softly laid a hand on Donny's neck,
To comfort, though, not willing to inspect.
"Rest easy now, good buddy. You'll be fine,"
He said, "The chopper'll be here in no time."
The angels held their breath to watch the act

As night gave way to starless inky black.

When Donny died they sent him to the flame,
And not a relative his ash would claim.
So in the parlor, sitting at a desk,
Sat Dude and Walter in their Tuesday best:
The Dude in just his bowling shirt and shades,
Then Walter in his surplus army-mades.
In silence there they sat in granite hall
And absently read scripture on the wall.
At long last did a funereal gent
Ascend the stairs behind their chairs' placement.
He took his seat behind the desk and sighed,
And took the men's attire all in stride.
"Hello there, gentlemen? You're the bereaved?"
He asked; his wormy voice popped th' air it cleaved.
"Yeah man," The Dude replied, all tired out,
Exhausted beyond grief and beyond pout.
He'd struggled with the weight of this ordeal;
Was too o'erwhelmed, it seemed, to simply feel.
"My name is Francis Donn'lly. Pleased to meet,"
The funeral director said to greet.
Then, "Jeff Lebowski", "Walter Sobchak" came,
"Though most the time, instead of my real name…"

Dude started with his bit to coolly hint
While digging through a dish of dinner mints.
"Excuse me?" Francis Donnelly inquired.
"Oh. Never mind," Dude said, and it expired;
As now was not the time for petty things
Like Dude's nickname, the casualness it brings.
This was a place for grieving and remorse,
And Dude was way too stoned to feel much worse.
Above this game of cleverness and feigns,
"I understand you're taking the remains?"
Was Donnelly's attempt to needle on
As tactfully as possible, these pawns.
So Walt said, "Yeah," with all its due respect.
"We have the urn," said Francis, "Card or check?"
As Francis got to business, out he held
A sort of leather folder, turtleshelled.
He chose a neutral spot to lay the tab
Between the two, for anyone to grab.
Again did Walter "Yeah" 's he took the bill
And held it as a lawyer holds a will.
Produced he reading glasses from his vest;
Around each ear they'd wrap, on nose they'd rest,
But halfway down his beak like some old man,
His head cocked back so he could ably scan.

As Walter read the details, Dude and Frank
Made eye contact though both faces were sank.
In silence Dude shot Donnelly a grin
And got back a mortician's smile from him.
At length then Walter raised the bill again
To place it on the desk and point with pen.
"What's this?" he asked the stooge to clarify
An errant charge that somehow caught his eye.
This Donnelly rotated the receipt,
But never bent a finger for the feat.
All palms like a magician handling decks,
He pawed the folder, craned his pencil neck.
"This charge is for the urn," he edified,
His eyelids raised, concerned brow creasing wide.
"Don't need it, Walter said, as calmness waned,
"We think we're gonna scatter the remains."
"Ah yes," said Donnelly, "You told us that.
Howe'er, of course, we'll simply need some vat
Or some receptacle to eas'ly pass
The whole of your departed loved one's ash."
Such treachery to cast on men so tired!
The Dude grew worried, Walter filled with ire.
"This's a hundred 'nd eighty dollars," Walter said,
Disturbed but somehow not losing his head.

Now Francis Donnelly seemed all nonplussed,
Uncomfortable that money was discussed.
"The urn," he said, "is actually quite nice,
And yet it is our most modestly priced."
The Dude and Walter each could ill afford
To cover both the urn and room and board.
Their bankruptcy a very acute threat,
They lived on cash and could not harbor debt.
"Can we just…" Dude began, but was cut short;
"A hundred eighty dollars?!" Walt'd retort.
So Donnelly, with fingers interwove,
Said, "They can cost three thousand or above."
The louder Walter got, the more he moved,
The more this Donnelly turned business-smooth.
"Can we just rent one?" Dude naively tried.
"We're not a rental house," said Francis, snide.
"We're scattering the fucking ashes, man!"
Screamed Walter, who was losing his élan.
The Dude would quiet him, but Walter snapped:
"JUST 'CAUSE WE'RE B'REAVED, IT DOESN'T MAKE US SAPS!"
"Please sir," said Francis, "try to low'r your voice,"
Concerned some other mourner'd regret their choice.
Still grasping for an answer, some win-win,

Dude asked, "D' you have naught else to put him in?"
But Donnelly, his nose turned up halfway,
Repeated, "That's the least you'll get to pay."
"Goddamnit!" Walter bellowed, slamming wood,
"Is there a Ralph's within this neighborhood?"

On windswept bluff above the endless sea,
The Dude and Walter processed solemnly.
First to the summit Walter did embark;
Beside and just behind Dude found his mark.
They'd bought a Folgers can for Don's remains,
Not some generic brand owned by the chains.
In Walter's hands the can glowed brightly red
With plastic blue sealed lid wrapped 'bout its head.
He held it at arm's length and faced it west
So that its passenger would be at rest.
Walt breathed in deep – 'twas such a gorgeous day! –
And smiled despite himself before he'd say,
"Donny was a good bowler, and a good man.
He w's one of us, despite our curséd plan.
He was a man who loved the great outdoors,
And bowling, as was ev'dent by his scores,
And as a surfer he explored each beach
That Southern California claims 'n its reach.

La Jolla, Leo C'rillo, Pismo, too.
None of these shores escaped his board's purview.
He died. He died as so many other men
Of his generation, 'fore he had said 'when.'
In your wisdom, Lord, you took our friend,
As you took so many other flow'ring men,
At Khe San, Lan Doc, Hill Three-Sixty-Four.
These young men give their lives to serve their corps.
So'd Donny. Donny who ... who loved to bowl.
We'll miss this man. We honor him. And so...
Donald – Theodore – Karabotsos. Friend.
In 'ccordance with what your wishes might have been,
We c'mmit your final, mortal dead remains
To the Pacific Ocean's briny mains.
The ocean which you loved so very well,"
He finished, patting Donny's tinny shell.
His eulogy presented, Walter peeled
The plastic lid away and ash revealed.
"Good night, sweet prince," he sadly then intoned
And shook the can to send his comrade home.
The windy angels blew the ash around
And behind Walter, 'ere it'd meet the ground,
A bit of it blew back to Hollywood,
But most of it clung squarely to The Dude.

Not mortified, but frozen into place,
A disappointed look graced Duder's face.
When Walter finished up his sacred chore
He breathed in and exhaled the grief he bore.
Walt bongoed on the can to clear it all,
Then noticed with a touch of grossed-out gall
That half a pinch of ash had caught his vest
Where gray flakes of his friend had laid to rest.
With knife of hand he brushed his shoulder off
As stoically Dude watched without a cough.
At length did Walter finally look back
To see his fuming friend had been ash-smacked.
"Oh shit. I'm sorry, Dude," Walt 'pologized,
And started brushing ash from beard to thighs.
"This goddamn wind," did dusting Walter winge,
As prev'sly stoic Dude became unhinged:
"Goddamnit, Walter!" did The Dude explode,
While smacking off Walt's hands like dusty foes.
"You fucking asshole!" screamed Dude angrily,
"Ev'rything with you's a fucking travesty!"
Through this Walt's "sorries" were outright profuse,
"It was an accident," but to no use,
For Dude, though dwarfed by this vet in his vest,
Shoved furiously hard on Walter's chest.

"And what about the shit 'bout Vietnam?"
Dude frantically exploded like a bomb,
"Please tell me what the fuck that has to do
With anything affecting me and you?"
"I'm sorry, Dude," was all that Walter'd say,
For th' first time lost, unraveled in dismay.
The Dude had never fought like this before;
What fruits of rage his pacifism bore!
"Shit Dude. I'm sorry," Walter's voice was hushed,
Apologizing for the years he pushed
And made his friend an underling instead
Of listening to what The Duder said.
"God, Walter. You're a fuck," Dude nearly cried,
Half for his rage, half for their friend who'd died.
Another, softer shove did Dude then land,
Affecting Walt to move with flattened hands.
The two men stood there stiff against the wind
When Walter raised his arms and leaned he in.
Still dazed, he held his friend in an embrace
And said, "Ah, fuck it," screwing up his face.
Stuck with this guy, resigned to keep his friend,
Exasperated, Dude picked up his hand
And clapped it on the broad of Walter's back,
Surrendering to end the hug/attack.

Thus Walter let him go with a withdrawal
And offered "Let's go bowling," to his pal.

CHAPTER XI

The bowling lane's so beautiful sometimes,
It seems no man could conjure its designs,
And if in symmetry some angel lives,
Then to a million angels, home it gives.
The wood itself as smooth as ice that froze
Within a lake where no wind ever blows,
Then all the mean machinery behind
That sets the pins in order every time.
A man could scatter every pin he saw
And still from chaos order would restore.
If angels are in light when it reflects,
Inside the charge that chills the victors' necks,

In every song that makes you tap your feet,
In every drink you drink and all you eat,
Sit on the head of every pin that's hit,
Then angels must be bowling, and that's it.
Back at the lane, The Dude came to the bar
In higher spirits than the angels are.
"Two more oat sodas, Gary," he'd request,
While taking piles of air into his chest.
"All right," said Gary, popping off two caps,
"Good luck tomorrow," said to Duder's back
As Dude was taking in the angels' sights.
"Hey, thanks man," Dude returned through muted lights.
"I'm sorry t' hear 'bout Donny,' Gary spake,
Which turned The Dude to chat during his break.
"Yeah, well, you know. Sometimes you eat the bar;
Sometimes…" The Dude began but trailed off far.
And just as he'd forgotten all the phrase,
The source of it, off to his west, did gaze.
The Dude beheld The Stranger, and likewise;
This man smiled, "Howdy do, Dude," with his eyes.
"Oh hey, how are ya?" Dude said to his friend,
"I wondered if I'd see you here again."
He turned to face the cowboy-dresséd man
And pawed some beer nuts idly with his hand.

The Stranger said, "I wouldn't miss the game.
How are things goin'?" in his drawl untamed.
"You know, man. Strikes and gutters. Ups and downs,"
Dude answered wearily, but not through frown.
The Stranger's eyes just crinkled as he smiled
And, "Sure. I gotcha," answered he all mild.
Then Gary, like two beams from some lost star,
Put down two gleaming bottles on the bar.
"Thanks, Gary," said The Dude, "I must get back.
Take care," he told The Stranger as he snacked.
"Oh sure," The Stranger said, and tugged his bill,
"You take her easy, Dude. I know you will."
"Yeah man," The Dude said turning, arms flung wide,
Responding, "Well, you know. The Dude abides."
The Dude had bowed a little and left out,
Downlane to Walter for Walt's beer did shout,
And left The Stranger hearing what he'd heard.
The Stranger spoke, and savored every word:
"The Dude abides. Well, I don't know 'bout you,
But I take comfort that that's what he'll do.
It's good to know he's out there. He, The Dude.
To take her easy for the sinnin' brood.
I sure hope he can make the finals, too.
I guess that's just 'bout does her. This thing's through.

It wraps her up, and I think things worked out
For Dude and Walter finishing their bout.
And Hell, it was a purt good story, right?
Sure made me laugh to make it through the night.
Well, parts, an'way. I din't like seeing Donny go.
But, then again, I just happen to know
That there's a li'l Lebowski on the way;
Just 'bout nine months to that varmint's birthday.
I guess that's how the human comedy
Perpetuates itself in harmony,
Down through the generations it goes flyin',
Westward the wagons, through the sands of time,
Until – Aw, Hell. I'm ramblin' again.
I just hope you enjoyed yourselves. The end."
The Stranger turned to Gary, flagged him down:
"Got anymore o' that sarsaparilla 'round?"

www.ingramcontent.com/pod-product-compliance
Lightning Source LLC
Chambersburg PA
CBHW031638040426
42453CB00006B/143